101 THINGS EVERY CHRISTIAN TEEN SHOULD KNOW

Knowing God, Trusting His Word, Living by Faith, Growing in Wisdom, Shaping Your Future, and More!

RILEY KEATON

ISBN: 978-1-962496-16-2

**For questions, please reach out to
Support@OakHarborPress.com**

Please consider leaving a review!

Just visit: OakHarborPress.com/Reviews

FREE BONUS

SCAN ME!

GET OUR NEXT BOOK FOR FREE!
Scan or go to:
OakHarborPress.com/Free

TABLE OF CONTENTS

INTRODUCTION

Welcome to *101 Things Every Christian Teen Should Know*. Whether you chose this book for yourself or received it as a gift, taking the time to learn more about God shows that you're already dedicated to your faith.

You'll probably recognize many of the topics in this guide. We'll review a variety of different ideas and give you the information you need to think about each concept in detail. Hopefully, this book will help you understand more about God and what it means to be a Christian.

HOW TO USE
THIS BOOK

Chronological order is best for your first read through. Each chapter contains a set of lessons centered around a core theme, such as the Holy Spirit or God's role in daily life. You'll also study key verses from the Bible and learn more about influential figures in Christianity.

Everyone reads at their own pace, so don't feel the need to rush. You can read one chapter per day or just pick up the book whenever you have a few minutes of free time. The important thing is to make sure you're in the right mindset to dedicate yourself to God and engage with what you're reading.

A Message to Young Christians

This guide contains 101 different lessons and topics to guide you in your faith, but that doesn't mean you should stop learning when you're finished. If a particular topic catches your interest, continue researching it on your own to see what else you can find. You may even want to bring it up at your youth Bible study or small group meeting to discuss it with other teens from your congregation.

It's natural to rethink your childhood opinions or change your mind as you get older. If you have a question in the future, you can revisit any of these sections to refresh your memory or read about other perspectives.

CHAPTER ONE: UNDERSTANDING GOD

God is eternal, omniscient, and everlasting. As humans, we aren't meant to fully understand God or what He has in store for us. All we can do is follow God's commands in the Bible and trust in Him to guide us.

With this in mind, it's still important to think about God and learn what we can about His wishes. Praying, reading the Bible, and speaking with other Christians are three key ways to expand our understanding of what God expects from us. Prayer is especially important for maintaining your personal connection with God.

[1]
GOD'S EXISTENCE:
WHY DO WE BELIEVE IN GOD?

Everyone has their own reason for believing in God. For many Christians, the universe itself is proof of God's existence. The world is so sophisticated that it seems unlikely it's just a matter of coincidence. After all, out of the entire galaxy, we're the only planet ever found that supports human life. That's pretty amazing, and it matches up with what the Bible says about creation.

Additionally, when you look at other creatures in nature, it's obvious that humans are different from other animals. It supports the idea that humans alone are made in God's image. We're special and capable of things that are far beyond even the most intelligent animals.

People also believe in God because they recognize the truth in the Bible. It explains many historical events that wouldn't otherwise make sense and includes famous stories that have been handed down for generations. When you're ready to hear God's call, the Bible becomes more than just words or a book. It's proof that God has continued to watch over humanity even in times when we doubted Him.

[2]
GOD'S NATURE: WHO IS GOD?

God is the creator of the universe and everything you see around you in the natural world. God is sometimes referred to as the Holy Trinity. Each person in the Holy Trinity represents a different aspect of God. If you think of the Holy Trinity as a triangle, each point is unique, but they're still part of the same shape.

God, the Father is the first person in the Holy Trinity. As the creator of the universe, God is Father to every living creature. He shares a special bond with humanity and guides us in the way that human parents guide their children. Even though we break the rules and don't always listen to what God commands, he still loves us.

God, the Son is the second person in the trinity. God sent His only Son, Jesus Christ, to save humanity from our sins. Jesus Christ came to live among us in human form. He taught humans how to follow God's will and seek God's forgiveness.

The Holy Spirit is the third person in the Holy Trinity. God carries out His work on Earth through the Holy Spirit. In John 3:6–8, Jesus explains, "Flesh gives birth to flesh, but the Spirit gives birth to spirit. You should not be surprised at my saying, 'You must be born again.' The wind blows wherever it pleases. You hear its sound, but you cannot tell where it comes from or where it is going. So it is with everyone born of the Spirit."

[3]
GOD'S ATTRIBUTES: LOVE, JUSTICE, OMNIPOTENCE

God has many attributes and characteristics. He is powerful, merciful, and wise. Yet, above all else, God is loving and compassionate. The greatest example of God's love is that He sent his only Son to save us and offer us a path to eternal life. He continues to encourage us to share in His love by accepting Jesus Christ and loving those around us.

God is also just and fair in all His decisions. Throughout history, God has punished humanity, but He never abandons us. Even when Adam and Eve broke the law by eating the forbidden fruit, God didn't turn His back on us. He understands that we'll make mistakes because He chose to give us the power of free will.

Because God is omniscient, He can see what's in our hearts. He knows our flaws and shortcomings. Instead of being embarrassed at the thought of God knowing everything about you, take comfort in the fact that He's been beside you for your entire life. You can share anything with God because of His enduring love for who you are as an individual.

[4]
GOD'S PLAN: UNDERSTANDING GOD'S PURPOSE FOR THE WORLD

God has always existed and will always exist. God's deep knowledge of the universe allows Him to create plans that we can't even imagine. That's why the events we see on Earth don't always make sense to us. God may focus on one event in the present that won't affect anything for hundreds of years.

God's plan includes each and every one of us. Sometimes, our plans for the future don't work out because they're different from what God intends. Proverbs 19:21 tells us, "Many are the plans in a person's heart, but it is the Lord's purpose that prevails." When your idea of the future suddenly changes, consider that it's God's hand guiding you to where you truly belong.

While it might be frustrating to lose a championship game or fail the test for your learner's permit, these setbacks are opportunities to show that you trust God's will. Maybe a failure or setback in your life was necessary to achieve a greater purpose.

[5]
GOD IN THE BIBLE:
AN OVERVIEW OF GOD'S ROLE
IN THE SCRIPTURES

The Bible is divided into the Old Testament and the New Testament. The Old Testament starts with the beginning of the universe. In Genesis, God takes on the role as creator while designing each creature and building the natural world.

As humans settle into civilizations and spread across the world, God shares his laws for humanity through a few chosen people. During this part of the Old Testament, we see God, the Father teaching His children and punishing those who insist on breaking the rules. In 2 Timothy 3:16–17, the Bible says, "All Scripture is God-breathed and is useful for teaching, rebuking, correcting and training in righteousness, so that the servant of God may be thoroughly equipped for every good work."

God also prepares humanity for the arrival of Jesus Christ, which leads into the New Testament. The New Testament tells the story of how Jesus fulfills the promise of the Messiah. It also focuses on Jesus spreading the Gospel and teaching His followers how to honor God. In this part of the Bible, we not only see God directly, but also learn more about Him through Jesus.

CHAPTER TWO:
BUILDING A RELATIONSHIP
WITH GOD

Cultivating a relationship with God is a life-changing experience. At first, it can be intimidating to speak directly to God, but there's no reason to be nervous. God created each of us and knows us better than anyone else. He's always listening and ready to have a deeper connection. James 4:8 says, "Draw near to God, and He will draw near to you."

Now that you're a teenager, you'll probably have new questions about your faith and what it means to serve God. It's completely normal to experience doubt or wonder whether God accepts the real you.

[6]
PRAYER:
HOW TO TALK TO GOD

In general, prayer is how we talk to God. Making prayer a habit ensures that you're consistently working on your personal relationship with God. Many Christians pray before they go to bed and reflect on what happened throughout the day. Other people prefer to pray in the morning to start their day off on a positive note. It's completely up to you and what makes you feel the most comfortable.

When you pray on your own, you don't need to worry about the exact words you use to communicate with God. You should always be respectful, but it's okay to use simple language and share whatever comes to mind. If your friend seemed upset at school, you might say, "Dear God, my friend is having a hard time lately. I'm not sure what to do to cheer her up. Please help her find peace, and please help me be a better friend."

In this scenario, you're telling God what's happening in your life and turning to Him for guidance. Talking to God like a friend or a loved one encourages you to be honest without stressing about saying the perfect words. God knows your voice and hears the true meaning behind what you have to say.

Different branches of Christianity, which are known as *denominations*, have their own unique views about prayer. Christians from some denominations also ask the Virgin Mary or individual saints to pray for them as well. For example, Catholics often recite the Hail Mary, which states, "Holy Mary, Mother of God, pray for us sinners, now and at the hour of our death."

[7]
LISTENING TO GOD:
HOW TO HEAR GOD'S VOICE

You can open yourself up to God no matter where you are. Many people find it easier to hear God when they're in church or surrounded by nature. If you feel closer to God in certain places, going there might help you quiet your inner voice and listen while you pray.

It's helpful to think of prayer as a conversation with God. In between sharing your own thoughts and feelings, make room to hear God's reply. As you form a closer relationship with God, it will get easier and easier to hear His voice. As Jesus says in John 8:47, "Whoever is of God hears the words of God."

If you're still having a hard time hearing God's voice, think about what's going on in your life. Are you really listening if you're stressing about a bad grade or thinking about your plans for the weekend? Letting go of worldly problems and allowing the peace of God's love to wash over you will help you hear His call.

[8]
READING THE BIBLE:
IMPORTANCE & TIPS

Reading the Bible allows us to connect with God and understand how to honor Him with our actions. There are countless ways to read the Bible based on your personal preferences and what feels right to you.

Instead of being organized in chronological order, the Bible is separated into categories based on the contents of each book. In total, the Bible contains 66 books and covers roughly 1,500 years. There are 39 books in the Old Testament and 27 books in the New Testament.

The simplest strategy is to read the Bible from start to finish. This method is best if you want to familiarize yourself with each section. You'll start with the Old Testament and the book of Genesis. The first books are about God's laws. From there, you'll learn about history, poetry, and prophets. In the New Testament, you'll discover the history of Jesus's life and the church. The New Testament also includes Paul's letters and letters by others.

Another approach is to read the Bible while searching for verses about a certain theme. If you're not sure whether you want to make up with a friend after an argument, looking for passages about friendship can help you make a decision. You may also discover related themes like forgiveness and love that play a role.

[9]
WORSHIP:
DIFFERENT WAYS TO
WORSHIP GOD

The most traditional way to worship God is by going to church, but that's not the only option. Praying at home, studying the Bible with a group, or going to Sunday school also keeps your focus on praising God. Worshipping alone and with a group are different experiences, so it's great to try a mix of both.

You can also show your gratitude to God when you're doing things that aren't necessarily religious. Throughout history, Christians have used the creative arts to worship God. Some of the most incredible paintings, songs, and statues were originally inspired by biblical stories. Do you recognize any of these?

- *The Last Supper* by Leonardo da Vinci
- *Messiah* by George Frideric Handel
- *Madonna della Pietà* by Michelangelo (di Lodovico Buonarroti Simoni)
- *The Tears of Saint Peter* by El Greco
- *Gates of Paradise* by Lorenzo Ghiberti

There are also plenty of modern artists and musicians who include religious themes in their work. In fact, that led to an entirely new genre of music: Christian rock. Newsboys, Skillet, and Switchfoot are just a few examples. Even if your church is more traditional, you can still celebrate God through music by singing hymns, joining the choir, or playing an instrument.

[10]
FAITH:
WHAT IT MEANS TO HAVE
FAITH IN GOD

Faith is the foundation of trust. Having faith in God goes beyond believing in His existence, reading the Bible, and praying. Faith is about completely accepting God's wisdom instead of picking and choosing what to follow. It also means that you're loyal to your commitment to God.

This verse from 1 John 4:16 shows that when we have faith in God, He has faith in us as well: "And so we know and rely on the love God has for us. God is love. Whoever lives in love lives in God, and God in them."

Faith is also about action and the decisions we make. When God made humans, He wanted us to have free will. Choosing to follow God's laws instead of giving in to sinful behavior is how we show our faithfulness and dedication.

[11]
TRUST:
LEARNING TO TRUST GOD
IN ALL CIRCUMSTANCES

Sometimes, it's difficult to understand why certain things happen. A tragedy might strike a good person while sparing others who are evil and selfish. Part of trusting God is accepting that everything is taking place according to His plan.

The Bible shows how God has earned the trust of Christians over the course of thousands of years. He didn't ask everyone to just believe in Him without reason. Instead, God proved that He was all-powerful and all-knowing by performing miracles. Gradually, Christians learned to trust God's strength and wisdom.

Trusting in God can help you feel less anxious about the future. No matter what happens, God will support you and show you the way forward. If you make a decision that you later regret, it doesn't mean you've changed the entire course of your life forever. God will guide you through any detours you might need to take to get back to where you're meant to be.

CHAPTER THREE:
GOD'S ROLE IN EVERYDAY LIFE

God is always watching over us. You don't need a special occasion to involve God in your daily life. Even if you're just watching TV with a friend or studying for your biology test, God is still there to guide you.

In many ways, it's comforting to know that God is near. You can reach out any time to share your thoughts or ask a question. Making prayer part of your regular routine encourages you to have a closer, deeper relationship with God.

[12]
GUIDANCE:
HOW GOD GUIDES US DAILY

Daily life is full of so many small decisions that you may not even realize how many choices you make throughout the day. From choosing a show on TV to deciding whether to take a nap, you're constantly making decisions that affect how your day turns out.

You also end up reacting to the choices others make while they're around you. For example, if your sister is in a bad mood and looking for something to eat, you might give in when she asks to have some of your ice cream. She chose to ask for your permission, and you get to decide whether or not to agree.

Sometimes, God isn't necessarily guiding us directly. If you give your sister permission to eat your ice cream because you want to be charitable and kind, then that's still God's influence showing through you. As Philippians 2:13 says, "...for it is God who works in you to will and to act in order to fulfill his good purpose."

[13]
MAKING DECISIONS:
SEEKING GOD'S WILL

Daily life is full of decisions that range from what to wear to how to spend your free time. You'll periodically encounter even bigger choices, such as which electives to take or whether you want to attend Bible camp over the summer. When you're stuck on a decision, praying can help you clear your mind and understand which path is the best according to God's plan.

Studying the Bible is another way to make decisions that meet God's expectations. Obviously, not everything will have a direct answer. The Bible won't comment directly on cell phones, junior prom, or whether you should go to a Christian college. However, you can still find relevant verses that apply to modern situations if you keep an open mind.

Talking to other Christians in your life can also help you understand your options. Your pastor, friend, or youth group leader might see another angle that you missed. Even if you don't agree with their suggestions, those conversations can still give you something else to think about when you're unsure about a decision.

[14]
FRIENDSHIPS:
CHOOSING FRIENDS WITH GOD'S GUIANCE

It might not seem like you chose your current friends, especially if your friendships happened naturally from spending time together in church, school, or your neighborhood. However, any kind of relationship takes work, and the ones you invest in are the ones you choose to continue. Every time you text a friend or invite them to come over, you're making that friendship even stronger.

Sometimes, you can figure out whether you've chosen the right friends just by thinking about whether they have similar values. Do they cheer for you to succeed once they know you have a goal in mind? Are they supportive of your faith? Answering these basic questions can help you see if a friendship is healthy and built on respect.

That doesn't mean all your friends need to be Christian. In fact, making friends with people from different religions is an important part of interfaith harmony and promoting peace. Someone can still be a positive influence in your life, even if they don't have the same religious beliefs.

Plus, you never know when your friends might take an interest in Christianity. After seeing your journey and learning more about God, a friend who isn't religious could decide to join you one day for a Sunday service. Remember that Jesus didn't shy away from spending time with sinners and nonbelievers. Instead, He tried to understand them so that He could show them the truth of God's love.

[15]
SCHOOL & WORK:
BRINGING GOD INTO YOUR LIFE

You probably already have a routine to ensure you spend enough time praying, studying the Bible, and going to church. However, taking tougher classes or starting a part-time job can disrupt your usual routines. You may need to adjust your usual schedule now that you're older. If you used to pray at 8 p.m., but you're staying out later for work, you can move your bedtime routine a little later.

Prayer and Bible study should never feel like chores. If you can't fully concentrate after a long day, consider waking up earlier to pray and read the Bible. The exact time doesn't matter. The important part is that you're opening yourself up to God and making Him an ongoing priority in your life.

Don't let yourself become so distracted by sports, homework, or your social life that you forget about your faith. It's challenging to juggle so many obligations at once, but your commitment to God shouldn't be up for negotiation. Learning how to bring God into your life at this age will help you form the right mindset as you become an adult with even more day-to-day responsibilities.

If you're having trouble making time for God in your life, be honest with Him about what you're going through. Share what you're feeling and ask for His guidance as you search for a routine that works. God will see that you're doing your best to make space for Him in your life as you adjust to a busier schedule.

[16]
HOBBIES & INTERESTS: HOW TO HONOR GOD WITH YOUR PASSIONS

When God designed you, He gave you different skills and abilities. Some teens are natural athletes, while others are talented at the arts. No matter what you enjoy doing, putting your passions to good use honors God by showing gratitude for your talents and interests.

Depending on your hobbies and skills, you might be able to use your passions to support your congregation. If you love drawing, volunteer to design posters for upcoming events like a church play. Once people are aware of your talents, they may even ask you to participate in events that match up with your skills. You can also meet up with leaders in your church to let them know you're interested in taking on more responsibility.

Being creative with your talents can also help you uncover new ways to lend a hand that aren't as obvious. While being a field hockey star doesn't have a lot in common with acting, it probably means that you're strong enough to carry props back to the storage room after the performance is over. Volunteering your talents for simple tasks allows you to contribute even if you can't commit to helping all the time.

[17]
HANDLING STRESS:
FINDING PEACE IN GOD

Being a teenager is a stressful experience. Not only are you going to high school and gaining more independence, but you're also closer to making major decisions about college or your future career. That's a lot of pressure to deal with at once.

When you're feeling overwhelmed, remember that God is always with you. You can reach out at any time, even if you're just saying a quick prayer in between classes. Knowing that you're not alone during a stressful time can be reassuring, especially if you don't feel like talking to friends or family about what's going on.

Leaning on God when you're stressed and praying for His support shows humility. As 1 Peter 5:10 says, "And the God of all grace, who called you to His eternal glory in Christ, after you have suffered a little while, will Himself restore you and make you strong, firm and steadfast."

CHAPTER FOUR:
CHRISTIAN VALUES & CHARACTER

As Christians, God expects us to do good deeds and have a positive impact on the world. The same values and traits won't come naturally to everyone. Someone who's patient and honest may still struggle to forgive others. Meanwhile, a Christian who forgives easily might have trouble showing courage.

It takes time to develop these values and figure out your own strengths and weaknesses. Once you know where you can improve, you'll be able to create a plan to work on your personal character. Admitting that you need to work on yourself is the first step.

[18]
HONESTY:
WHY IT'S IMPORTANT
TO GOD

Honesty is important to God because it shows that you're dependable and true to your word. According to Proverbs 12:22, "The Lord detests lying lips, but He delights in people who are trustworthy." If you lie to others, you aren't respecting the truth and doing all you can to be a good person.

Lying also keeps you from admitting your own flaws. If you lie to escape the consequences of your actions, you're missing out on the chance to learn and grow as a person. Others may also stop trusting you if they realize that you're dishonest. Even if you're only telling "white lies," it still shows that you don't prioritize being truthful.

When you're willing to admit that you're wrong, you have an opportunity to change your ways for the better. In Luke 19:1–10, the tax collector Zacchaeus climbs a tree to see Jesus above a crowd. Back then, tax collectors were seen as dishonest and greedy, but Jesus decided to visit Zacchaeus's house anyway. After spending time with Jesus, Zacchaeus decided to change his ways and pay back anyone he'd cheated.

In this story, Zacchaeus learns to be honest about his behavior and admits that he hurt others. He also takes steps to repair his relationships with people from his past. This shows that it's always possible to grow as a person and become more honest.

[19]
KINDNESS:
REFLECTING GOD'S LOVE

Everyone knows that God is capable of punishing humanity, but Christians don't follow God out of fear. It's God's love that draws us together to worship Him. As Christians, showing kindness to others reflects God's love for us and makes the world a more welcoming place for everyone.

Being kind doesn't need to involve huge gestures. Small actions, such as picking up an item someone dropped or offering to take a teammate home after practice, can still make a difference. Showing kindness may also convince other people to pay it forward in the future.

The idea of performing random acts of kindness has become more popular in recent years. Random acts of kindness are spontaneous choices we make to brighten another person's day. One common act is to pay for a stranger's coffee, but there aren't any rules or limits. If you see the chance to reflect God's love, don't hesitate to spread kindness and put someone else's happiness before your own.

When you're being kind to someone else, make sure you're doing it for the right reason. You shouldn't help people just to get attention or praise. If your actions are selfish, then you're not really looking out for the other person's well-being.

[20]
HUMILITY:
UNDERSTANDING ITS
SIGNIFICANCE

Being humble is different from having low self-esteem. Humility doesn't stop you from being confident or believing in yourself. The key is to remember that you aren't better than anyone else just because you have certain skills, qualities, or possessions.

Remember that even Jesus was quick to show humility. At the Last Supper, there weren't servants around to wash the disciples' feet, so Jesus did it instead. He wanted to teach the disciples about serving others and staying humble.

Everyone might know that you're the smartest kid in class or the best cheerleader at a competition. Showing off only boosts your ego and makes it more likely that you'll become arrogant. When you reach a high level of skill, you should focus on improving your personal best and teaching others who are still learning.

For example, Simone Biles Owens is the most decorated gymnast of all time. Instead of bragging or seeking out attention, she's been humble about her achievements and used her success to help her fellow gymnasts. Biles invited her Olympic teammate Jordan Chiles to train in Texas at a time when Chiles was thinking about quitting the sport altogether. It turned Chiles's career around and allowed her to stay in competition.

With her humility and gratitude, it's no surprise that Simone Biles is a Christian. Not only is she open about her faith, but she also credits God with giving her the strength and talent to succeed. As you can see, being humble can remind you to look beyond your own efforts and recognize that reaching your goals takes support from friends, family, and God.

[21]
PATIENCE: TRUSTING GOD'S TIMING

Everything happens on its own timeline according to God's plan. God has always existed, even before He created the universe. His sense of time is different than ours because our lives are so short by comparison. While it may seem like you've been waiting forever for something to happen, God knows when the time is right. He doesn't rush just because we're impatient to reach a goal or start a new phase of our lives.

There are also cases in the Bible where God has given instructions or rules to humanity without fully explaining what's about to take place. It's up to us to trust God's timing. For example, when God spoke to Noah and told him to build the ark, Noah didn't know the exact reason or how long it would take to complete. He trusted God and got to work on his task. In the end, it took him 120 years to build the ark and collect all the animals that went inside.

[22]
COURAGE: STANDING FIRM IN FAITH

Courage is about facing your fears and standing up for what you believe in. Part of that courage is being willing to stand by God even when other people question your faith. Not everyone believes in God, and you'll probably meet at least a few people who try to convince you that God isn't real.

God understands that leading a godly life takes dedication. After Moses's death, God spoke to Joshua and told him several times to be strong and courageous as he led the Israelites into the Land of Canaan. God also reassured Joshua that He would be with them wherever they went. That promise also applies to all of us. If you're afraid or it's hard to find the courage to stand up to others, God is there to help you stay strong.

Everyone has their own doubts and fears, so courage is also extremely personal. There will be times when you need to overcome your fear in order to serve God. If you're terrified of public speaking, then the idea of reading Bible verses out loud in Sunday school could require courage. Others might be able to do the same thing without any hesitation but struggle later when they encounter a different type of challenge.

Instead of worrying about how you look to other people, think about your own journey. Have you had the courage to stand up for your faith? Are you willing to face your fears to become a better Christian? Asking yourself these questions will help you see how you can improve instead of staying in your comfort zone.

[23]
FORGIVENESS:
LEARNING TO FORGIVE
AS GOD FORGIVES

God is willing to forgive even the most serious mistakes. When Moses went up the mountain after leading the Israelites out of Egypt, the Israelites were afraid he was lost forever. Aaron created a golden calf for them to worship instead.

God was angry at them for abandoning His teachings and turning to idols instead. He told Moses to go down the mountain and said that He would destroy the Israelites who worshipped the golden calf. Moses begged God to spare them, and God forgave the Israelites.

This story is just one example of God's mercy. Even though the Israelites insulted and disobeyed Him, God decided to forgive them and fulfill the promises He had already made. Later, Jesus continued to spread a message of forgiveness to His disciples.

In Luke 6:37, Jesus says, "Judge not, and you will not be judged; condemn not, and you will not be condemned; forgive, and you will be forgiven." He also reminds us that it's easy to love and do good for people who offer the same effort in return, but we should care for everyone regardless of how they respond.

Jesus wants us to forgive others even if they don't apologize or acknowledge what they did wrong. It takes hard work to get to the point where you can freely forgive your enemies. Keep in mind that forgiving someone doesn't mean accepting or approving of their behavior. If another kid bullies you in school, you can forgive them while still taking steps to protect yourself.

Forgiveness leaves the door open to change your relationship in the future. Someone who was mean to you in the past might decide to apologize later if they think you're willing to listen. When you forgive others, you'll also have a better understanding of what it takes to earn forgiveness when you've hurt someone else's feelings.

Ultimately, you can't control how other people act. All you can do is change your reaction. Instead of getting angry and letting a bully ruin your day, forgiving them in your heart frees you from those negative emotions. It can also help you clear your mind as you think about what to do next.

CHAPTER FIVE: UNDERSTANDING JESUS

God sent Jesus to redeem humanity and save us from the sin that entered the world when Adam and Eve ate the forbidden fruit. Sacrificing Jesus for our sins is one of God's greatest acts of love. Through Jesus's death, God created a New Covenant with humanity to replace the one that was broken.

[24]
WHO IS JESUS?:
UNDERSTANDING HIS IDENTITY

Before Jesus was born, the angel Gabriel went to Galilee to tell the Virgin Mary that she had been chosen by God to conceive the Son of the Most High. Jesus was born in Bethlehem, but He grew up in Nazareth.

Jesus was raised in a large family, along with Mary and Joseph's children. Even from a young age, He was a fast learner who was wise beyond His years. According to Luke 2, Jesus stayed in Jerusalem after the family traveled there to observe the Festival of Passover. Mary and Joseph didn't realize He was missing from their caravan home until an entire day had passed. Since Jesus was only 12 years old, they rushed back to Jerusalem to search for Him.

After two more days, they finally found Jesus at the temple courts. He was speaking with the teachers and asking them questions. When Mary asked Him why He had stayed behind, Jesus replied, "Why were you searching for me? Didn't you know I had to be in my Father's house?"

This story highlights how Jesus was deeply connected to both God and the everyday people around Him. It's also a hint into how Jesus continues to strengthen the relationship between God and humanity. Timothy 2:5-6 says, "...there is one God and one mediator between God and mankind, the man Christ Jesus, who gave Himself as a ransom for all people."

[25]
JESUS'S TEACHINGS:
KEY LESSONS FROM HIS LIFE

Many of Jesus's lessons take the form of parables. These stories each contain an important message about God or what it means to be a Christian. For instance, a legal expert once asked Jesus, "And who is my neighbor?" Jesus explained in Luke 10:30–35 by telling the story of the Good Samaritan.

In this parable, a man was traveling from Jerusalem to Jericho when he was attacked by thieves. They took his clothes and beat him before leaving him in the street. A priest and a Levite both passed him by on the other side of the road. A Samaritan, however, stopped and helped the man. He treated his wounds and brought him to an inn in town to recover.

After sharing this story, Jesus asked the legal expert which one of the people was a neighbor of the injured traveler. The man replied that it was the Samaritan since he'd shown mercy to the traveler. Jesus confirmed that his answer was correct and said, "Go and do likewise."

The parable of the Good Samaritan is just one example. Researchers don't always agree on how many parables are in the Bible, but there are at least 30. Besides the Good Samaritan, the most famous parables include:

- The Sower
- The Prodigal Son
- The Lost Sheep
- The Mustard Seed
- The Rich Man and Lazarus

Each of these parables contains its own theme and message. Jesus's teachings often focused on returning to God, helping others, and loving one another. Some of His lessons are commonly shared in daily life, even among people who aren't Christian. For example, you might have heard the Golden Rule that states to "treat others as you would want to be treated." Compare that saying to Matthew 7:12: "So in everything, do to others what you would have them do to you, for this sums up the Law and the Prophets."

[26]
THE CROSS:
THE SIGNIFICANCE OF
JESUS'S SACRIFICE

Jesus died on the cross to save humanity and pay for our sins. As Matthew 20:28 says, "…the Son of Man did not come to be served, but to serve, and to give his life as a ransom for many." Through His death, we can see how much God truly loves us. Instead of punishing humanity for eternity, He sent His Son to bring us forgiveness and mercy.

Jesus gave us the promise of eternal life by repairing our relationship with God and freeing us from sin. 1 Peter 3:18 says, "For Christ also suffered once for sins, the righteous for the unrighteous, to bring you to God." Now, we all have the ability to reach Heaven through our choices and our faith.

[27]
RESURRECTION:
WHY IT MATTERS

The resurrection fulfills Jesus's promise that He would rise again. When His disciples realized that the tomb was empty, they knew beyond the shadow of a doubt that everything Jesus had said was true. It built trust with all who followed Jesus and convinced many people that He really was the Son of God.

Without the resurrection, the early Church might not have survived. Hundreds of witnesses testified that they had seen Jesus resurrected from the dead. Those who hadn't met Jesus in life still recognized the resurrection as the work of God. The story quickly spread as more and more people became Christian and committed themselves to serving God.

The resurrection also showed that God accepted Jesus's sacrifice as payment for humanity's sins in the Garden of Eden. 1 Corinthians 15:21–22 says, "For since death came through a man, the resurrection of the dead comes also through a man. For as in Adam all die, so in Christ all will be made alive."

[28]
SALVATION:
WHAT IT MEANS FOR US

Salvation means that we have been saved from sin by Jesus's death and resurrection. As Christians, we earn our salvation through faith. Since we have free will, the only way to fully embrace our faith is to repent for our sins and change for the better. It's a case of actions speaking louder than words.

If that seems confusing, think of the same idea in terms of your personal relationships. Imagine that you're part of a group project in school. One of the members never responds to texts and doesn't turn in their work. When you confront them about it, they promise to be better, but they don't actually change their behavior. How much does their apology mean if they don't try harder in the future?

CHAPTER SIX:
THE HOLY SPIRIT

Along with God, the Father and God, the Son, the Holy Spirit makes up the final person in the Holy Trinity. He guides us and helps us understand how to serve God. In John 10:15–17, Jesus explains, "If you love me, keep my commands. And I will ask the Father, and He will give you another advocate to help you and be with you forever — the Spirit of truth."

[29]
WHO IS THE HOLY SPIRIT?: UNDERSTANDING HIS ROLE

The Holy Spirit is God's power and influence in the world. He lives in the heart of every Christian who has true faith in God. During tough times, the Holy Spirit guides and protects us. He gives us the strength we need to follow the right path, even when we aren't sure of what might happen next.

The Holy Spirit also teaches us and helps us understand God's word in Scripture. He uses the Bible to influence our decisions and show us what we need to change to become better Christians. As 2 Timothy 3:16–17 says, "All Scripture is God-breathed and is useful for teaching, rebuking, correcting and training in righteousness, so that the servant of God may be thoroughly equipped for every good work."

[30]
FRUIT OF THE SPIRIT: DEVELOPING CHRISTIAN CHARACTER

The Fruit of the Spirit includes nine traits that appear when someone lives in harmony with the Holy Spirit. Paul lists these in Galatians 5:22–23:

- Love
- Joy
- Peace

- Forbearance
- Kindness
- Goodness
- Faithfulness
- Gentleness
- Self-control

When you recognize these qualities in people, you'll know that the Holy Spirit is at work in their lives. Many Christians believe that love is the most important because it leads to the other fruits. When you love others, it's easy to show them kindness and gentleness. Love for God also brings joy, peace, and faithfulness.

If you don't have some of these traits, think about what you can do to open yourself up to the Holy Spirit. For example, if you want to work on joy, make a plan for what to do the next time you start to have negative thoughts. This could be as simple as taking a minute to pray and refocus on all the positives in your life. With hard work and the power of the Spirit, you can improve your personal character to be closer to what God expects.

[31]
GIFTS OF THE SPIRIT: RECOGNIZING & USING THEM

The Holy Spirit gives different gifts to each of us. When we work together, our gifts allow us to do more together than we could ever accomplish apart. Isaiah 11:1–2 explains that there are seven gifts of the Spirit:

1. Wisdom
2. Understanding
3. Counsel
4. Fortitude
5. Knowledge
6. Piety
7. Fear of the Lord

Each person receives the gifts of the Spirit in their own way. If you're having trouble recognizing your gifts, it's often helpful to ask someone else. Other people might be able to point out qualities or traits you don't notice in yourself.

Once you're aware of your gifts, think of how you can use them to support your community and honor God. Using your strengths will allow you to accomplish even more in God's name than if you try to imitate what others are doing. Romans 12:6–7 says, "We have different gifts, according to the grace given to each of us. If your gift is prophesying, then prophesy in accordance with your faith; if it is serving, then serve; if it is teaching, then teach."

[32]
LIVING BY THE SPIRIT:
DAILY GUIDANCE & EMPOWERMENT

Living by the Spirit is about being open to God's influence and developing your own relationship with God. Instead of only thinking about what you want from day to day, staying connected to the Spirit means that you're also considering God's teachings, rules, and expectations.

Listening to the Spirit and reading the Bible will also help you stay strong against temptation. For example, if you're tempted to lie to get out of trouble, your faith will remind you to be honest about your mistakes. When you're willing to listen, the Holy Spirit can guide you away from sin and closer to a godly life.

CHAPTER SEVEN:
THE CHURCH

Christianity is made up of more than just one church or denomination. Christians originally belonged to the same group, but different people had their own opinions about how to interpret the Scripture and honor God. Over time, these disagreements caused Christianity to expand into multiple different branches.

The first split took place in the 11th century when the Eastern Orthodox churches broke away from Catholicism during the Great Schism. Instead of following the Pope, Eastern Orthodox churches are led by bishops under the direction of the archbishop of Constantinople.

Another split occurred in the 16th century during the Reformation. In 1517, a German monk named Martin Luther challenged the way the Catholic Church was handling the forgiveness of sins. He criticized the sale of indulgences, which allowed people to purchase certificates in exchange for forgiveness. In Luther's eyes, the only way to earn forgiveness was to have faith in God and properly atone for breaking God's laws.

Once Luther criticized the Church, others started to doubt whether Catholicism was the right way to worship. Anyone who separated from the Catholic Church became known as a Protestant. From there, Protestants created their own denominations and churches. Lutherans, Methodists, Baptists, and Anglicans are all Protestants.

In modern times, most countries with a large population of Christians have a mix of denominations. Catholicism is the dominant group, followed by the Southern Baptist Convention, the United Methodist Church, and The Church of God in Christ.

[33]
WHAT IS THE CHURCH?
ITS PURPOSE & FUNCTION

The purpose of the church is to worship God, welcome new Christians to the faith, and help people live as God intends. For Christians, the church is a place to gather and meet others who follow God. Since most people go to church nearby, it's also a way to make local connections with other people from the same community.

Beyond the local level, the various branches of Christianity have their own leadership structures. The simplest model is a hierarchy with a single leader at the top. For instance, the Pope is the head of the Catholic Church. He interprets the Bible, offers guidance on modern issues, and makes decisions about the future of the Church.

Other churches are governed by a group of elected leaders. These individuals make decisions together and support local churches in their communities. The Presbyterian Church in America (PCA) is an example of this type of system. The PCA is governed by the General Assembly, which meets once per year to discuss the most important issues facing the Church. Each region chooses its own representatives to attend.

Independent churches that don't belong to a wider network may also have a congregational structure. In these types of churches, everyone in the congregation has a vote. Some independent churches still have leaders in key roles, but they can remove officials at any time as long as a majority of the congregation agrees.

[34]
BEING PART OF A CHURCH: FINDING YOUR PLACE

Belonging to a congregation is an amazing experience. It's like having a second family to support you and guide you in your faith. Some churches only serve a small community, while others have hundreds of members.

At your age, you probably belong to the church your parents or guardians attend. Once you're an adult, you may decide to join a different church or even switch to another denomination. Some people discover that they'd rather belong to another branch of

Christianity, especially if they're marrying someone from another denomination.

The most important factor is whether you feel comfortable and supported. If you don't have a strong connection to your church, it'll be harder to work on your relationship with God and build ties within the congregation. Churches also have their own views and priorities that won't always align with yours.

For example, you may feel happiest in a church with thriving small groups and a congregation that hosts a variety of different activities. If you belong to a church where you're one of the only young people, switching to a church that includes more social support could help you come out of your shell.

In many cases, you can also encourage change from within your existing church. That's an easier approach if you love your congregation but dislike certain parts of how the church operates. Expressing your ideas to leaders shows that you're committed to the church and interested in adding new programs, events, or groups.

[35]
SERVICE & MINISTRY: WAYS TO SERVE GOD

There are countless ways to serve God based on your skills and talents. Even if you don't want to become a pastor or priest, you can still contribute to the church and make God a central aspect of your life. As 1 Corinthians 12:5 says, "There are different ways to serve. But they all come from the same Lord."

The religious leaders in your church can help you take on more responsibility when you're ready. You could serve as a greeter during services or hang up posters for an upcoming event. If you're too busy with school, sports, or work to volunteer on a regular basis, look for opportunities to help others whenever you're at church. For example, if you see someone cleaning up after Bible study, grab a broom or a trash can to lend a hand.

Another way to serve God is by being a positive influence in your local area. Potential options include volunteering at a shelter or cleaning up a nearby park. You may also have neighbors who need help from time to time. Offering to shovel snow or cut someone's grass could make a huge impact on someone else's well-being.

You'll also find unexpected opportunities to serve God in your everyday life. Whether it's refusing to help another student cheat in class or encouraging a teammate during a tough practice, you're serving God anytime you make personal choices based on what you think He would want you to do. Even if no one else sees that you're doing the right thing, God will still know.

As you get older, you'll start thinking more seriously about the future and what you want to do for a living. It's possible that you'll decide to serve God in a more official capacity as a priest or pastor. In that case, the first step is to apply to college. Most applicants to a seminary already have a bachelor's degree.

Students who intend to go to a seminary earn their bachelor's degrees in a variety of different fields. Philosophy and history are popular options, but you might feel drawn to math, biology, or another technical major. College is your chance to pursue your own interests, and there's no single major that will prepare you for seminary better than any other.

[36]
COMMUNITY:
THE IMPORTANCE OF
CHRISTIAN FELLOWSHIP

Christian fellowship is the connection between all people who believe in God. Every time you pray or worship, you're joining millions of other Christians around the world. Even if you don't have anything else in common with another Christian, you'll still have an unbreakable bond through God.

In the early days of Christianity, Jesus's followers worked together to support one another. They put aside their differences and shared whatever they had as one community. In 1 Corinthians 12:12–13, Paul says, "Just as a body, though one, has many parts, but all its many parts form one body, so it is with Christ. For we were all baptized by one Spirit so as to form one body—whether Jews or Gentiles, slave or free—and we were all given the one Spirit to drink."

Christian fellowship is the foundation of a healthy congregation. You don't have to get along with everyone, but you should still respect them as a member of your Christian family. If you know that someone is sick, unhappy, or going through another problem in their personal life, reach out to see what you can do to help. Just think of the Parable of the Good Samaritan. Uplifting the people around you follows Jesus's teachings and lets you grow closer to the other Christians in your life.

CHAPTER EIGHT:
CHALLENGES & QUESTIONS

Faith comes with its own challenges. As you gain more life experience and think about your future, you'll most likely have new questions about God. Don't be ashamed if you feel doubt or uncertainty. It's completely normal to wonder if everything you believe is true.

In fact, it's healthy to admit when you're struggling and work your way through it. If you never acknowledge that you have doubt, you're not being honest about your faith. Avoiding the problem and trying to convince yourself that everything is fine will only cause you even more stress.

Plus, working through your doubts will eventually make your faith even stronger. When you're tempted to make a bad decision or other people try to change your mind, you'll already have the answers you need to say no.

[37]
DOUBT:
HANDLING DOUBTS
ABOUT FAITH

Believe it or not, experiencing doubt is a part of faith. It's a test of what you really believe, especially as you set out on your own and learn to think beyond what you were taught as a young child. Overcoming your doubts and fears will take time.

Instead of feeling guilty or trying to force yourself not to have doubts, think about why you're experiencing those emotions. You might have questions that you need to answer before you feel more secure in your faith. There may also be ideas or opinions that you don't agree with. Learning more about your beliefs will help you have a deeper understanding of God.

When the disciples doubted the resurrection, Jesus wasn't angry. He showed them patience and kindness when He appeared to them. According to Luke 24:38, "He said to them, 'Why are you troubled, and why do doubts rise in your minds?'" Jesus showed them His hands and feet to convince them that He had risen.

Similarly, Jesus was never upset when His followers asked questions or had moments of weakness. There were also many times that He performed miracles to prove that He really was the Son of God. These events show that Jesus has always been understanding about doubt and those who need time to accept Him as the Messiah.

[38]
SUFFERING: UNDERSTANDING WHY IT HAPPENS

Bad things happen every day, and it's natural to question why God allows people to suffer when He has the power to intervene. In many cases, suffering happens because God gave us free will and the ability to make our own choices. Other people's decisions affect what happens in everyday life, and God can't interfere without taking away their free will.

God also has a plan for everything that's meant to happen. We can't see everything that God takes into account when He sets a plan in motion. If someone is suffering, it could be that God wanted to teach them a new way of seeing the world. After all, going through hard times can help us be more compassionate and loving toward others.

There are also times when God lets us fail because we didn't follow His rules. In fact, this is how we learn a lot of basic lessons as children. If your dad tells you to wear knee pads and you ignore him, it's not his fault if you fall off your skateboard and scrape your knee. The next time you want to go skating, you'll probably think twice before you ignore your dad's advice.

Accepting that bad things can still be part of God's plan shows that you trust in His wisdom. You may still be angry that your grandmother is in the hospital, or your best friend broke his arm, but you can't change what's happening without going against what God knows is best.

[39]
TEMPTATION: OVERCOMING IT WITH GOD'S HELP

Temptation is a test of your commitment and faith. When you're faced with the option of committing a sin, you'll sometimes feel pulled to do the wrong thing. You might even try to talk yourself into it. From shoplifting in a store to being jealous of your sibling, the things you find tempting will vary based on your personality.

Fortunately, it's possible to overcome temptation through willpower and dedication. If you find yourself being tempted, removing yourself from the situation and praying about what happened can help you understand more about your weaknesses. While you pray, be honest with God about what you experienced. Temptation happens to everyone, and you shouldn't be ashamed about sharing your faults with God.

Saying no the first time can be one of the hardest steps. After that, you've already proven that you can resist temptation. You can also change your habits to make sure that you aren't in the same position again. For example, if you're tempted to spread gossip, stop your friends when they start sharing a rumor with you. If you never hear the rumor in the first place, then you won't be tempted to gossip.

[40]
PEER PRESSURE: STAYING TRUE TO GOD

Peer pressure is everywhere. Whether it's spending time with teammates at practice or waiting in line at a store, there are always social expectations about how to act. You can't completely ignore these pressures without being rude. Some amount of peer pressure is usually a good thing because it helps people be nicer and more respectful to each other in society.

There are also expectations about how to be a good Christian. When you teach someone else about God or show them how to behave, you're using positive peer pressure. In that case, it isn't just about helping another person fit in at your church. You're actually showing them how to stay true to God.

Unfortunately, not everyone will have your best interests at heart. Other people might pressure you to do things that are against your beliefs. When that happens, remember to keep your priorities in the right order. Your commitment to God is more important than looking cool to your friends or trying the latest viral challenge online. When other people are pressuring you in a harmful way, remember this passage from Proverbs 13:20: "Walk with the wise and become wise, for a companion of fools suffers harm."

Everyone makes mistakes, and if you give in to negative peer pressure, do your best to get back on the right path as soon as possible. Avoid situations where you might be tempted to do the same thing again. God understands that we will sin and break the rules from time to time. The important thing is that you eventually realize you're heading in the wrong direction.

[41]
SCIENCE & FAITH:
HOW THEY CAN COEXIST

It's true that science and faith don't always agree, but that doesn't mean you need to choose between one or the other. Some of the world's most famous scientists have devoted themselves to both God and science. Gregor Mendel, the father of genetics, was a priest. George Washington Carver, most commonly known for inventing peanut butter, felt that his scientific research was inspired by God. These are just two examples from throughout history.

Many people interpret the Bible in different ways. The same applies to scientific principles. There isn't always a clear answer, and it's natural to have questions. If your religious values and scientific principles don't seem to line up, remember that our understanding of science is always changing. Back in the day, people believed that the sun revolved around the Earth. Now, we know differently.

You won't be able to know the truth about everything. Part of faith is sticking to what you believe, even when it's hard. If you're having trouble balancing faith and science, researching how famous scientists viewed both may be comforting. You can also set aside time to pray on it and share your thoughts with God.

[42]
OTHER RELIGIONS: RESPECTING EVERYONE

When you meet people who follow other religions, treat them with love and respect. Just because they have different beliefs doesn't mean you can't be friends or search for things you have in common. Even the Catholic Church says that Christians can learn from people who believe in other faiths. According to the Church, non-Christians can still be a "secret presence of God" when they show truth, grace, and other Christian qualities throughout their lives.

As you learn more about world religions, you'll also see that many other faiths recognize Jesus in some way. Islam, for instance, views Jesus as one of God's messengers. Even though Muslims don't accept that Jesus is the Son of God, they still have some beliefs that overlap with Christianity.

When you meet people who follow other faiths, do your best to listen. Their ideas and religious stories will be different, but you shouldn't take it as an attack on your beliefs. It's possible to respect each other even if you don't agree with the other person's religious values. The same is true if you meet someone from a different denomination of Christianity. You might think your denomination is the right way to worship God, but it's not your job to criticize someone else's beliefs.

Respecting everyone, regardless of their religion, is known as *interfaith harmony*. In fact, the United Nations even recognizes a special week dedicated to fostering respect between religions. World Interfaith Harmony Week takes place every year in February. During this week, leaders from all over the world work together to show respect for all religions and beliefs.

CHAPTER NINE: LIVING OUT YOUR FAITH

Faith is a huge part of who you are as a person. It's natural to want to share that with others. The way you live out your faith is unique to you. Every Christian has their own ideas, interests, and talents. While there are a lot of activities that are designed for groups, there are also plenty of opportunities to show leadership on your own.

At your age, it's a great idea to experiment with different programs and projects. You never know when you might discover a passion for singing in the choir or helping younger kids in Sunday school. Don't be afraid to try new things. Even if you don't stick with a certain program or hobby, it doesn't mean you failed. You're simply learning how to share your faith in a way that feels right.

[43]
EVANGELISM:
SHARING YOUR FAITH

Evangelism is the act of spreading the Gospel and sharing your faith in Jesus Christ with others. Many people convert to Christianity after learning about Jesus from their friends or family. 2 Corinthians 5:20 says, "We are therefore Christ's ambassadors, as though God were making his appeal through us. We implore you on Christ's behalf: Be reconciled to God."

Another way to help people embrace Christ's love is by setting a good example in your everyday life. When people see how happy and fulfilled you are, they'll be more willing to listen to what you have to say about God. Even if someone doesn't want to become a Christian when you talk to them the first time, you might be planting the seeds for them to convert in the future.

Remember to be respectful whenever you're talking about your faith. The goal isn't to bully anyone into converting or pressure friends to come to church with you. Believing in Jesus is a choice that everyone has to make for themselves. You can give them the information, but you can't force anyone to become Christian. God gave humans free will for a reason. That also means that people have the free will to follow their own religions and beliefs.

[44]
MISSIONS:
UNDERSTANDING GLOBAL
MISSION WORK

Mission trips are another way to spread the word of God. They involve traveling to other countries to teach people about God and perform community service. Many mission trips are open to high schoolers as long as you're of a certain minimum age.

Your church may have a relationship with other churches around the world, or they might plan mission trips to different locations every time. Traveling with other members of your congregation can help you feel comfortable as you leave the country, potentially for the first time. There are also third-party groups that organize trips and host volunteers from multiple churches.

Depending on your destination, a mission trip can cost hundreds or even thousands of dollars per person. You may need to volunteer and raise funds before you can go on a mission trip. Besides the direct costs of the mission, you'll also have individual expenses such as getting a passport, taking language lessons, or buying luggage. Your congregation should have a plan laid out to guide you through each part of the process.

Going on a mission trip gives you the chance to learn about different cultures and gain a better understanding of how you want to serve God. Christians in other countries will have their own cultural traditions that are different from yours. It can be amazing to see how many ways there are to worship God.

If a mission trip really inspires you and fills you with purpose, then it could be part of your personal calling. 1 Peter 4:10 says, "Each of you should use whatever gift you have received to serve others, as faithful stewards of God's grace in its various forms." You might want to look into taking another trip or research careers that allow you to continue supporting people around the world.

On the other hand, it's perfectly alright if you decide against going on a mission trip. For example, if the thought of traveling to another country makes you nervous or you can't miss that much school, you can still support the mission from home. You could help others raise funds or spread awareness about the trip within your congregation. Every little bit contributes to the same goals.

[45]
SOCIAL JUSTICE:
GOD'S HEART FOR JUSTICE

Social justice is about fighting for what's right and fair in society. You don't need to be a Christian to support social justice, but many values overlap in both circles. A lot of social problems are complicated, so you'll need to take time to understand how you feel. Issues such as climate change, racial equality, feminism, healthcare, and poverty are all part of social justice.

As you can see, these topics are far from simple, and there isn't always a clear answer about what's morally right. For example, if you think the criminal justice system doesn't always do the best job of deciding who's innocent, what's the alternative? How would you fix things if you could?

Asking yourself these questions makes it easier to decide when to take action and how. If you realize that poverty is hurting your local community, you could set up a toy drive through your church or donate food to a shelter. Getting involved is a great way to share God's love for others while making society a better place. You might even realize that you want to fight for social justice as part of your career.

When you're not sure what God would want you to do, it's okay to stay undecided. Praying can give you time to think about social problems and work through your feelings with God. Reading the Bible can also help you see issues from a different point of view. You don't have to agree with what others say about social topics.

It's more important to follow your heart and listen to what God wants you to do.

[46]
ENVIRONMENTAL STEWARDSHIP: CARING FOR GOD'S CREATION

God created everything in the natural world. It only makes sense that we should protect it and show our appreciation for the plants, animals, and places around us. In fact, when God first made humans, He wanted us to be caretakers for the land and His creatures. One of our first responsibilities was to look after God's creations.

Obviously, you won't be able to take care of the entire planet by yourself. However, you can make small changes in your daily life to reduce your impact on the Earth. You've probably learned about recycling in school, but if you don't already know what's recyclable, do some research to see what you can recycle in your area. Your parents or guardians may also have more information about what items your local recycling facilities will accept.

Besides recycling, think about how much trash you make and why. Could you donate a shirt you don't like anymore instead of throwing it away? Are there disposable items that you could replace with reusable ones? Reducing the amount of trash that goes into landfills helps the environment and the animals who depend on natural habitats.

Taking care of the natural world could also involve helping animals in need. Volunteering at an animal rescue gives you the chance to spend time with animals while also supporting your local community. If school or sports takes up too much of your time to volunteer on regular basis, you can still offer to take a dog on a walk or make a donation to the shelter.

[47]
GENEROSITY:
LIVING A GENEROUS LIFE

Generosity is about giving back to others instead of only thinking about yourself. You don't need to make huge gestures or give away all your possessions to have a positive impact on those around you. Even small acts of kindness and generosity can make the world a better place.

When you give to others, don't just donate things you don't want anymore. Giving away something of value is completely different from giving away an item you don't care about. Mark 12:41–12:44 tells the story of how Jesus saw people donating money to the temple in Jerusalem. Wealthy people gave a lot of money without much thought because they had so much extra to spare. A poor woman, however, could only afford to give two small coins. Jesus told the disciples that the woman was more generous because she gave money even though she needed it.

Therefore, when you give away your time, money, or energy, try to do it for the right reasons. Being generous is about giving without expecting or wanting anything in return. If you're only helping someone because you want compliments or praise, then you're actually being selfish. Before you take action, stop and think through the entire situation, including your personal motivations.

It's okay to set boundaries on how much you give. If you're exhausted and your sibling asks you for help, you don't need to drop everything to support them just because they asked. Most people will be understanding if you explain that you have other things going on. You might say, "Gym class was really hard today. I'm wiped. Can we do this later, after I take a nap?" You can't give generously if you don't take care of yourself, too.

[48]
LEADERSHIP:
BEING A CHRISTIAN LEADER

Even as a teenager, there are plenty of chances to become a leader in your church. You could volunteer to take on roles in your youth group or during Sunday school. If there aren't any positions available, ask if there's some way you can give back by taking on more responsibility.

Even if you don't take a formal leadership role where you're in charge, you can still take more responsibility in other ways. When you set up chairs for youth Bible study or help a friend who's having a bad day, you're showing leadership by setting a good example.

Participating in local service projects is another way to show leadership. If your church doesn't have any community service on the calendar, volunteer to take a lead role in planning a new activity. It doesn't have to be a major event. Just cleaning up a park or collecting canned goods for a shelter gives you a chance to give back and take initiative.

As you get more experience, you can expand onto bigger projects and pursue more challenging leadership opportunities. It's okay to start small and gain some confidence in your abilities. Remember to keep learning from your mistakes and trying new things as you go. Eventually, you might feel ready to go on a mission trip or attend a conference away from home.

CHAPTER TEN:
PREPARING FOR THE FUTURE

As a teen, you're moving through the period in between childhood and adulthood. You'll have a lot of decisions to make at this stage of your life. One of the biggest decisions is choosing a future career path and what you want to do after high school. A lot of teenagers go away to college, but you might want to learn a trade, start working right away, or take a year off.

Besides school, you'll also need to adapt and learn new skills as you get older. Hopefully, your parents or caregivers will continue to support you in the future, but you'll eventually become more independent as you start your adult life. Don't be too hard on yourself as you do things for the first time. No one expects you to be an expert in relationships, taxes, or a new career.

This can be a confusing time in your life. If you feel pressured or rushed, remember that you have an entire congregation ready to support you. Don't be embarrassed or shy about asking for advice. Every adult you know from church has been in your shoes. They can answer your questions, make suggestions, or just listen while you explain what you're going through.

[49]
CHOOSING A CAREER:
SEEKING GOD'S GUIDANCE

Choosing a career is a huge decision. Careers in fields like medicine or law require years of study, so you need to prepare as early as possible. Thinking about your natural talents is a great starting point. God designed you in a special way with unique characteristics and skills. While you don't need to use your talents for work, many people follow their passions while trying to earn a living.

God has a plan for everyone, and He will guide you in the right direction. Sometimes, a career won't end up being the most important thing in your adult life. Your calling might be to volunteer in an unpaid role or raise a family. Money isn't everything, so don't stress if there isn't a career that jumps out to you right away.

Even people who love their jobs still have other passions and interests. For instance, pretend that you want to be a veterinarian. After you graduate from college and start working, being a vet won't suddenly take over your entire personality. You'll still have your faith and your loved ones. Therefore, while choosing a career is a big deal, it isn't the only decision that affects who you are.

[50]
RELATIONSHIPS:
GODLY DATING & MARRIAGE

You may have already started dating, but even if you haven't, it never hurts to plan ahead for the future. When you're looking for a relationship, try to find someone who appreciates your values and your religion. Someone who doesn't support your faith could tempt you into making bad decisions that you'll only regret later.

You don't need to get married right away, but every date is a stepping stone to learning what you want in a serious relationship. Start small and listen to your heart. Invite a classmate to a dance or plan a double date with friends at the movies. As you go on more dates, you'll start to figure out what you're hoping to find in another person. Do you want someone who makes you laugh? Does your ideal partner have the same interests and hobbies?

You've most likely already heard this passage from 1 Corinthians 13:4–7 that describes the power of love: "Love is patient, love is kind. It does not envy, it does not boast, it is not proud. It does not dishonor others, it is not self-seeking, it is not easily angered, it keeps no record of wrongs. Love does not delight in evil but rejoices with the truth. It always protects, always trusts, always hopes, always perseveres." Above all else, your future marriage should be this type of love that honors God.

[51]
FINANCES:
BIBLICAL PRINCIPLES FOR
MANAGING MONEY

Even if you don't have regular income from a part-time job, you should take the time to learn about managing your money. This way, it won't be a shock when you do start earning a paycheck and paying for your own expenses. Not only will this make it easier to save up for important purchases, but you'll also understand more about the Bible's view on money.

Using money is unavoidable. It's part of our society, whether you're buying lunch at school or paying tuition for college. However, your relationship with money also matters. While money is important, worrying about it too much will only make you selfish and greedy. Your goal should be to make enough for a good life without hoarding money just to say you have it.

Ecclesiastes 5:10 says, "Whoever loves money never has enough; whoever loves wealth is never satisfied with their income." Money isn't a measure of your success in life or how much you matter. Instead of focusing on getting rich, invest your time and energy into more fulfilling areas such as family and faith.

One simple way to manage your finances in a healthy way is by following the 50-30-20 rule. With this method, you spend 50 percent of your money on things you need and 30 percent on things you want. The remaining 20 percent goes into savings. The key is to make sure you're being honest about what you really *need* to spend money on.

If you have expenses that you pay every month, make a simple budget to keep your spending under control. This way, you'll know to set aside money for time with friends or a donation to your church. Resist the temptation to dip into your savings if you miscalculate. Your savings are the future or unexpected events that you couldn't predict in advance. While you won't have a lot of emergencies at your age, it's still a good habit to practice responsible money management.

[52]
LIFE GOALS:
SETTING & ACHIEVING THEM
WITH GOD

Your life goals are totally unique to you. God has a purpose for all of us based on our talents and experiences. People are called to many different walks of life. Instead of focusing on what others are doing, pray to God and ask Him to guide you to where you belong. Proverbs 3:5–6 says, "Trust in the Lord with all your heart and lean not on your own understanding; in all your ways submit to him, and he will make your paths straight."

As you're setting goals in your life, think about the answers to these questions:

- What makes you feel happy and fulfilled?
- Which jobs and careers sound the most appealing?
- When you daydream about the future, what do you think about?
- What gives you a sense of purpose?

You can't hear God's call if you don't take the time to listen. While some people have a natural talent that leads them to an obvious career path, that isn't true for everyone. Most Christians set life goals by praying, thinking through their options, and putting in the work to understand what God wants.

[53]
LEAVING HOME: STAYING CONNECTED TO GOD

Leaving home is a big step toward independence and your adult life. Moving into your own place or going to college can disrupt many of the routines you've developed to support your relationship with God.

You'll have a lot of decisions to make once you get set up at your new home. Where will you sit to read the Bible? When will you pray? You don't have to keep all your habits the same now that you're more in control of your schedule.

If you want or need to join a different church that's closer to your new home, don't rush into a decision. Take the time to look at various churches and talk to members of the congregation. Attending services at multiple churches can help you understand more about each before you settle on the right one. If you're a student, ask whether there's a chapel on campus. Many universities offer services, and you'll hopefully already have some friends who attend.

It also helps to make friends with people who value their faith. They might have different beliefs than you but spending time with others who understand your commitment to God can make it easier to prioritize your religion.

CHAPTER ELEVEN: DEEPENING YOUR FAITH

Your faith will grow and change as you get older. The views you have about society and the world aren't set in stone. In fact, it would be strange if you had the same opinions at 12 years old, 20 years old, and 85 years old. Change shows that you're still thinking about how to be a good Christian and follow the path that God has laid out for you.

Major life events such as moving away from home, getting married, or having children will disrupt your usual routines. You'll need to make all kinds of decisions and juggle different priorities. If that sounds intimidating, remember that you've already gone through so many stages of your life. When you were in elementary school, the idea of going to middle school probably felt scary. But now that you're older, you see that you made it through just fine.

[54]
BIBLE STUDY: GOING DEEPER INTO GOD'S WORD

There's always more to understand about the Bible. Think about the aspects you don't know well or haven't studied in detail. Visiting these parts again can help you learn something new and see the Bible from a different perspective. If you don't fully understand a certain idea, ask someone you trust for help or bring it up in your usual Bible study.

Studying the Bible isn't like learning a subject in school. You should try to learn everything you can and pay attention even to the most challenging passages. The Bible is so much more than just the most famous stories, but you won't get to experience it all unless you make an effort.

When you're facing a problem or a new stage of life, consider doing a targeted Bible study. This involves reading passages that focus on a certain topic that's important to you. A quick online search will show you where to find important verses and stories that relate to whatever is going on in your life.

For example, David is famous for defeating Goliath and later becoming king, but he also had a great friendship with Jonathan, the son of King Saul. If you're working through some issues with your friends, you might be interested to read more about their story. Other important friendships include the bond between Naomi and Ruth and how Job's friends supported him when he was in need.

[55]
MEMORIZING SCRIPTURE: WHY & HOW TO DO IT

When you memorize a piece of information, it's usually because you feel it's important and valuable to your life. From your phone number to the fastest route to get to math class, you probably have all sorts of details memorized that you don't think about consciously on a daily basis.

Many people memorize their favorite Bible verses. When you're stressed, being able to think through your favorite verses can help you relax. Knowing parts of the Bible by heart also allows you to connect with God even if you aren't in a place where you can pray out loud.

Memorizing a Bible verse is just like learning anything else you need to know off the top of your head. Here's one of the simplest methods:

1. Choose a verse or passage you want to learn.
2. Write the first one down on an index card or a piece of paper.
3. Read the verse out loud several times.
4. Turn the index card over and try to recite the verse from memory.
5. Check to see how close you were to the actual verse.

It will take a while to memorize long passages. You may need to spend multiple days working on it before you get it right. Keep the index cards even after you've learned a verse. This way, you can always go back to review if you need to jog your memory later.

[56]
PERSONAL DEVOTION: CREATING A QUIET TIME ROUTINE

Sitting quietly by yourself gives you time to think about who you are and what's going on in your life. Between school, after-school activities, and church, you're probably juggling multiple responsibilities at once. When you're busy, it can feel refreshing to have nothing to do except think and look back on recent events.

Consider setting aside a specific window of time to use for personal devotion every day. You can pray, think about anything that's bothering you, and take a few minutes to sit quietly. Make this a predictable part of your routine and try not to skip it even if you have other things going on.

Not only will this help you make God a priority in your life, but it will also ensure that you're resting enough throughout the day. Having quiet time before bed can be especially beneficial for your health. Instead of looking at devices or working on hobbies that keep you alert, reading the Bible or praying are both peaceful activities. They'll make it easier for you to drift off to sleep and feel content.

[57]
SPIRITUAL MENTORSHIP: FINDING A MENTOR

A spiritual mentor is there to support you in your faith. They answer questions and guide you when you're feeling lost. Sometimes, your mentor will be someone in an official role. This could include your pastor, a godparent, or your Confirmation sponsor.

However, any spiritual adult in your life can become your mentor. While it's easier to connect with someone in your congregation, your mentor could belong to another church entirely. For example, you may have a neighbor or a relative who enjoys praying with you and studying the Bible.

Unlike mentors who aren't religious, a spiritual mentor fully understands your commitment to God. If you need advice about something like applying to college, a spiritual mentor will understand that your faith plays a role in that decision. It's reassuring to know that someone is always there to stick up for you and help you work through anything that's bothering you.

Having a mentor might even inspire you to become a mentor in the future. This could be as simple as volunteering with younger kids in Sunday school or teaching others about major milestones like First Communion.

[58]
CHRISTIAN BOOKS: RECOMMENDED READINGS

Since you're reading this right now, you're obviously interested in Christian books. There are a lot of different options for you to choose from next, and most bookstores have at least a small section dedicated to Christian reading. Here are just a few ideas to help you get started:

- *This Changes Everything: How the Gospel Transforms the Teen Years* is unique because it was written by a teenager. Author Jaquelle Crowe was inspired to help other teens become better Christians. She talks about what it means to follow Jesus as a teenager and form the right spiritual habits.

- *The Jesus I Wish I Knew in High School* includes personal stories from 30 different authors. This book covers important topics such as school, relationships, and sin.
- *10 Questions Every Teen Should Ask (and Answer) about Christianity* by Rebecca McLaughlin tackles tough ideas and encourages you to think deeply about your faith. It explores the answers to questions such as *How can we believe the Bible is true?*

You can also look online for teen Bibles and devotionals that have extra content to guide you as you read. Daily devotionals for teens feature a different reading every day. Using a devotional is a great way to discover new parts of the Bible that you haven't studied in detail.

[59]
SPIRITUAL RETREATS: IMPORTANCE & HOW TO PLAN ONE

Spiritual retreats help you learn more about yourself and your faith in a peaceful environment. Instead of going to church for part of the day or reading the Bible at night after school, you'll have a whole block of time just dedicated to God.

Many spiritual retreats encourage you to leave your devices behind or limit how often you use them. You may still need to check in with family or use technology for an activity, but your goal should be to focus on your faith instead of other obligations. School, sports, and friends will still be there when you get back.

The first step is to decide when and where to hold your retreat. While there isn't a set time limit for these types of events, it's common to at least stay overnight. Scheduling a retreat over the weekend usually makes the most sense since people will have off from work and school.

A spiritual retreat doesn't need to be far away. Setting up sleeping bags in a meeting room at the church is a simple option that doesn't require travel. Holding your retreat at church also makes sense if you're inviting younger children who may feel nervous about sleeping in a new place away from home.

Depending on where you live, there may be state or national parks nearby that offer group campsites. Renting a group campsite for your retreat is a fantastic way to spend more time in nature while reconnecting with God and other members of your church. If that doesn't work, find out whether anyone in your congregation owns a farm or a large plot of land. You may be able to host your retreat on their property.

Once you have these basic details worked out, you'll need to get chaperones and plan activities. Make a sign-up sheet to hang up in church or ask specific people if you know they'll be interested in attending. Activities don't have to be complicated. Your schedule could be as simple as planning group meals, setting aside time for Bible study, and finding a game everyone will enjoy.

You don't have to plan the entire event by yourself. Ask the adults in your life for their thoughts and opinions. They may notice something you overlooked or have some suggestions to make your retreat go smoothly. It's especially helpful if you can chat with someone who's planned a successful retreat in the past.

74

CHAPTER TWELVE: INFLUENTIAL FIGURES IN CHRISTIANITY

From Moses to the disciples, you probably know many of the influential figures from the Bible. Studying the Bible in greater detail gives you the chance to learn more about their lives and the lesser-known people from their time. These leaders helped lay the foundation for modern Christianity and the church as we know it.

There are also current-day heroes and other influential Christians from throughout history that you should know. Missionaries, writers, and ordinary Christians have accomplished amazing things that are worth remembering and celebrating in modern times.

[60]
BIBLICAL FIGURES:
LEARNING FROM THEIR LIVES

One of the most important lessons to learn from biblical figures is that they weren't perfect. Bible stories often talk about mistakes people made and what they did to earn forgiveness from God and their loved ones. For example, Paul was once known as Saul of Tarsus. He was against Jesus and hunted down His followers to throw them in prison. Eventually, he met Jesus and realized that he was wrong.

In 1 Timothy 1:16, Paul says, "But for that very reason I was shown mercy so that in me, the worst of sinners, Christ Jesus might display His immense patience as an example for those who would believe in Him and receive eternal life." These types of stories prove that you can always change your bad habits and become a better Christian.

There are also incredible people in the Bible who put their faith above all else. When God warned Noah about the flood, he didn't hesitate to build the ark and follow God's instructions. Even though everyone around him was ignoring God and living sinfully, Noah didn't give in to temptation. He listened to God and trusted Him even though he didn't fully understand what God had planned.

As you can see, biblical figures faced tough choices and a lot of uncertainty, but the people who put their faith in God were never disappointment. God always followed through on His promises. These stories show that you can still trust in God even if you don't fully understand what's happening or why.

[61]
CHURCH FATHERS:
THEIR CONTRIBUTIONS TO FAITH

The Church Fathers are a group of individuals who helped establish Christianity and make the faith into what it is today. Some of them learned from Jesus's closest disciples, while others changed the path of the church hundreds of years later.

Pope Clement I was ordained by St. Peter and became the fourth Pope. He wrote a letter to the Corinthians to call for order after the Christians in Corinth removed their church elders from power. The letter became known as the First Epistle of Clement and was included in some Bibles in the New Testament.

St. Justin Martyr was born around the year 100 AD. He wrote several texts defending Christianity even though it was dangerous to be Christian at that time. He also went to Rome and started a school. After another philosopher betrayed him to the authorities, St. Justin refused to honor the Roman gods. He said, "No right-minded person forsakes the truth for falsehood." In response, the Romans executed St. Justin and six other Christians.

Two centuries later, Pope Damasus I became the bishop of Rome in the year 366 AD. He led the Council of Rome, which decided writings would be officially accepted by the Roman Catholic Church. Pope Damasus I was also known for trying to repair the relationship between Rome and Christian leaders in Antioch.

In roughly the same time period, St. John Chrysostom was born in Antioch in the year 347 AD. He would go on to become the Archbishop of Constantinople. During his life, St. John Chrysostom stood up against corruption in the church and targeted wealthy clergy who were abusing their authority. Instead, he took the savings and invested in projects like hospitals that would help the poor.

St. John Chrysostom is quoted as saying, "It is foolishness and a public madness to fill the cupboards with clothing and allow men who are created in God's image and likeness to stand naked and trembling with the cold so that they can hardly hold themselves upright." His message didn't sit well with the rich and powerful people in Constantinople. They eventually banished him, and he died in exile in 407 AD.

This isn't a complete list. There are over a dozen Church Fathers from different periods in history. If you decide to research them in greater detail, you might also see the Church Fathers divided into groups by where or when they lived.

[62]
MODERN-DAY HEROES: INSPIRATIONAL CONTEMPORARY CHRISTIANS

While it's incredible to read about all the Christians who helped build the early church, you should also take the time to learn about modern-day heroes. These leaders didn't hesitate to spread God's message and do everything they could to inspire others.

Saint Mother Teresa was born in 1910 in the Ottoman Empire, but she spent a large part of her life in India. While there, she founded the Order of the Missionaries of Charity to help poor people around the world. The nuns opened schools, orphanages, and hospitals. In 1979, Saint Mother Teresa was awarded the Nobel Peace Prize for her lifelong dedication to helping others.

Another modern-day hero is Reverend Martin Luther King Jr. King, who was born in Atlanta in 1929. Throughout his life, he advocated for equal rights for Black Americans and encouraged nonviolent forms of protest. He also served as the head of the

Southern Christian Leadership Conference. King was assassinated in 1968.

Other modern-day heroes weren't nuns or members of the clergy. They just felt called to do great things and spread love in the world. One of these people was Dorothy Day. Day was a writer and social activist. She wasn't religious in her early life, but she converted to Catholicism in 1927 after the birth of her daughter.

Day helped found the Catholic Worker Movement during the Great Depression. She supported the poor and better working conditions for ordinary people. When Pope Francis spoke about her life in 2015, he said, "Her social activism, her passion for justice and for the cause of the oppressed, were inspired by the Gospel, her faith, and the example of the saints."

Remember that Christians don't need to be famous to be significant. Anyone who inspires you to be a better Christian can be a hero to you. This could include a mentor at church or even someone in your family. Every Christian who tries to uplift and support others is helping the next generation of future leaders.

[63]
CHRISTIAN AUTHORS: INFLUENTIAL WRITERS & THEIR WORKS

Over the years, many Christians have written about their beliefs and commented on faith as a whole. Anselm of Canterbury was a monk and writer who became the Archbishop of Canterbury in 1093. He wrote *Why the God-Man?* and *Faith Seeking Understanding*. He also created a set of prayers and meditations that Christians could use in private to create a deeper relationship with God.

However, not every famous Christian author wrote directly about Christianity. For example, Jane Austen is world famous for her novels, which include *Pride and Prejudice* and *Sense and Sensibility*.

She was born in 1775, but her books are still popular to this day. You may have even read some of her work in school.

Austen's father and two brothers were reverends, and her faith was an important part of life. She's famously quoted as writing, "Incline us Oh God! to think humbly of ourselves, to be severe only in the examination of our own conduct, to consider our fellow-creatures with kindness, and to judge of all they say and do with that charity which we would desire from them ourselves."

Another famous Christian author is C.S. Lewis, whose works include *Mere Christianity* and *The Chronicles of Narnia*. Lewis was born in Belfast, Northern Ireland, in 1898. He believed that Christians shouldn't follow God's rules just because they want a reward. He wrote, "Thus if you have really handed yourself over to Him, it must follow that you are trying to obey Him. But trying in a new way, a less worried way. Not doing these things in order to be saved, but because He has begun to save you already."

Well-known Christian writers aren't limited to the West. Shūsaku Endō, the author of *Silence* and *Wonderful Fool*, was born in Tokyo in 1923. He converted to Catholicism as a child, even though Christianity wasn't popular in Japan at that time. His novel *Silence* follows a group of missionaries in the 17th century and explores the history of Christianity in Japan.

If you're interested in reading books by any of these authors, you may be able to find them at your school or community library. Your church may also have its own lending library of books by Christian authors. Don't hesitate to ask around if you need help finding something to read.

[64]
MISSIONARIES: THEIR IMPACT ON THE WORLD

Missionaries travel to other areas to spread God's message and help local communities. They continue with the work Jesus gave to the first apostles in Matthew 28:19–20 when He said, "Therefore go and make disciples of all nations, baptizing them in the name of the Father and of the Son and of the Holy Spirit, and teaching them to obey everything I have commanded you."

In the first years after the death of Jesus, the disciples traveled throughout the ancient world. Mark went to Egypt, while Paul preached in Western Anatolia. Missionaries eventually spread Christianity throughout Asia, Europe, and Africa, but it was most popular with powerful people like royals.

Teaching ordinary people about Christianity became easier after the invention of the printing press in 1440. The printing press made it cheaper to print Bibles and translate them into other languages. Education was also improving, which meant that more people learned how to read the Bible for themselves.

William Carey is often called the "father of modern missions." He arrived in India in late 1793 and began preaching. Over the course of several years, he translated the Bible into Bengali, which made it possible for people in India to learn about Christianity in their own language. In total, he spent 41 years working in India and welcoming new Christians to the faith.

David Livingstone was another famous missionary who journeyed from Scotland to Africa in 1841. Before leaving for Africa, he studied medicine for two years to make himself more useful to the London Missionary Society. Livingstone traveled all over the continent while spreading the Gospel. During that time, he became an accomplished explorer and used his experiences to speak out against slavery.

Mary Slessor had a difficult childhood, but she admired Livingstone's work in Africa. In 1875, she volunteered as a missionary and went to Calabar to follow in Livingstone's footsteps. While there, she started learning local languages and teaching the people she met about the Bible. She fought for women's rights and looked after abandoned babies. Slessor once said, "Christ sent me to preach the Gospel, and He will look after the results."

CHAPTER THIRTEEN:
HISTORICAL & CULTURAL CONTEXT

Christianity is an important part of world history. Even though religion is often separate from politics and the government, Christianity has played a huge role in how countries formed and expanded. For instance, the United States was settled by Puritans who wanted more religious freedom.

In modern times, Christianity is broken down into dozens of denominations. Many Christian traditions are also influenced by local cultures. It's especially common for different countries to have their own beliefs, festivals, and ideas about worship.

[65]
HISTORY OF CHRISTIANITY: MAJOR EVENTS & DEVELOPMENTS

In the early years of Christianity, the Catholic Church was the only major denomination. St. Peter traveled to Rome and became the first Pope. He was followed by St. Linus, then St. Anacletus. But as time went on, not everyone agreed with how the Vatican wanted things to be done.

Many Eastern churches disagreed with Western churches about everything, from which bread was acceptable for Communion to how much authority the Pope should have. This led to years of infighting between the two groups.

In 1054, Pope Leo IX excommunicated the patriarch of Constantinople, causing the Great Schism. The Great Schism marks the point that the Eastern Orthodox churches formally separated from the Catholic Church. Tensions only grew worse after Crusaders destroyed most of Constantinople in 1204.

The next significant split took place in 1517 when a monk named Martin Luther wrote a list of 95 theses and nailed them to the door of a church in Wittenberg, Germany. Luther's 95 theses criticized some of the practices of the Catholic Church. One of the main topics was the sale of indulgences.

At that time, people could buy indulgences to receive forgiveness for their sins. This meant that wealthy Christians could sin without worry since they had money to spare for indulgences. Martin Luther didn't believe that people should be able to "buy" their salvation. Before long, other people started to agree with him and question why indulgences were being sold.

In the summer of 1520, Pope Leo X said that 41 sentences in Luther's writings were heretical and against the teachings of the Catholic Church. He gave Luther 60 days to take back his words and admit that he was wrong. When the time limit was up, Luther took a copy of Pope Leo X's order and burned it. The Pope excommunicated him in January 1521.

Under the laws of the Catholic Church, heretics could be burned at the stake. However, local leaders in Germany felt that Luther deserved a fair hearing before he could be punished as a heretic. During the hearing, one report claims that Luther said, "I cannot and will not recant anything, for to go against conscience is neither right nor safe. Here I stand, I can do no other, so help me God."

On his way home, soldiers sent by a local ruler named Frederick III of Saxony intercepted to protect Luther. They brought him to a castle in secret to give him a place to hide. While there, Luther translated the Bible into ordinary German. This supported one of his most controversial beliefs — that Christians could understand the Bible for themselves.

Many people agreed with Luther's ideas. Protestantism gained even more support after King Henry VIII separated from the Catholic Church in 1534 after the Pope refused to annul his marriage to Catherine of Aragon. Instead, King Henry created the Church of England and had the Archbishop of Canterbury annul the marriage. This allowed the king to marry Anne Boleyn.

Protestants and Catholics continued to disagree and fight for power. The Thirty Years' War broke out in 1618 when Emperor Ferdinand II banned Protestantism within the Holy Roman Empire. Although the war was centered in Germany, other European nations joined the fight as the war carried on. By the time both sides agreed to peace in 1648, the war had claimed the lives of over eight million people.

The next significant historical milestone in Christianity took place in 1962 when the Vatican convened a council of 2,400 bishops. Their goal was to guide the Catholic Church into the modern age and update the official views of the Church. The council emphasized that the Church was made up of a network of bishops and the Pope instead of viewing it as a hierarchy under one person in power. It also established a more accepting view of other religions and Christian denominations.

[66]
DIFFERENT DENOMINATIONS: UNDERSTANDING THE DIVERSITY WITHIN CHRISTIANITY

Christianity is divided into multiple groups that have slightly different beliefs and traditions. There are thousands of denominations, some with only a few members. The largest groups are Catholic, Protestant, and Eastern Orthodox.

Catholicism was the first denomination to form within Christianity. Catholics follow the direction of the Pope and look to the Vatican for major decisions about Christianity. There are over 1.3 billion Catholics around the world, making Catholicism the largest single denomination.

Protestantism dates back to 1517 and the Reformation. Over time, more Christians split from the Catholic Church and formed their own denominations as Protestants. Nowadays, the majority of Christians in United States are Protestant. The largest Protestant denominations include Episcopal, Baptist, Methodist, Lutheran, and Presbyterian churches.

Eastern Orthodox churches fall into the same group, but they're all considered separate. Instead of following the Pope, each of the 17 churches has its own bishop who serves as leader. The Patriarch of

Constantinople represents the entire network of churches, but he isn't in charge. Instead, they refer to the Patriarch of Constantinople as "first among equals."

If you're interested in differences between denominations, you might be able to attend a different church with a relative or a friend. Visiting other churches gives you the chance to learn about new traditions and understand what makes each denomination unique. Remember to be respectful while you're a guest in another church. You don't have to agree with everything you see, but you should keep an open mind and thank the person who brought you.

[67]
CHRISTIAN HOLIDAYS: THEIR MEANINGS & TRADITIONS

Christian holidays are spread throughout the entire year, but the first major holidays take place in the days leading up to Easter. Ash Wednesday is in February or March and marks the start of Lent.

Lent is the 40-day period when Christians honor Jesus's sacrifice and remember the 40 days He wandered in the wilderness before the crucifixion. Christians often choose to give up something of value during Lent. For example, you could decide not to eat dessert for 40 days. Your church's exact traditions will vary based on your denomination. Catholics usually don't eat meat on Fridays during Lent.

The last week of Lent is known as Holy Week. On Palm Sunday, Christians remember when Jesus arrived in Jerusalem for the last time. His followers waved palm branches to welcome Him to the city. Many churches host a special service on Palm Sunday and hand out palms.

Good Friday is two days before Easter. It marks the day of Jesus's death. This is a time to reflect on how Jesus sacrificed himself to save humanity from sin. With his death, Jesus made it possible for humans to earn God's forgiveness and receive the promise of eternal life.

The exact date of Easter changes from year to year. It falls on the first Sunday after the spring equinox and a full moon. Easter Sunday remembers the resurrection of Jesus Christ after the crucifixion. Some churches host an overnight vigil leading into Easter, while others have special services in the morning.

Easter represents a fresh start and a new relationship between God and humanity. It's a time to celebrate God's love. 1 Peter 3 says, "Praise be to the God and Father of our Lord Jesus Christ! In His great mercy He has given us new birth into a living hope through the resurrection of Jesus Christ from the dead."

Easter also gives you the chance to welcome new members to your congregation. People who want to convert to Christianity are often baptized during Easter since they weren't baptized as babies. Your church may also invite the local community to celebrate.

After Easter, the next major holiday is Pentecost. This holiday celebrates the Holy Spirit appearing to Mary and the disciples. The Holy Spirit gave them gifts that allowed them to share the Good News about Jesus Christ. They could even speak other languages to make sure everyone who had gathered could easily understand them.

Peter convinced the crowd that the Holy Spirit had appeared to them and shared the news about Jesus. He told them, "Repent and be baptized, every one of you, in the name of Jesus Christ for the forgiveness of your sins. And you will receive the gift of the Holy Spirit." That day, thousands of people joined the church as new Christians.

The next set of major holidays isn't until the fall. All Saints' Day takes place on November 1. Christians celebrate this occasion by honoring the saints. All Souls' Day is November 2, and many people go to the cemetery to pay their respects to loved ones who have already passed on.

Lastly, Christmas takes place on December 25 to celebrate the birth of Jesus. Most schools and places of business close on Christmas Eve and Christmas Day. This is a great time to get more involved in your church to help with celebrations and any special services. Most Christians also exchange gifts and visit with family during this time.

[68]
CHRISTIAN SYMBOLS: UNDERSTANDING THEIR SIGNIFICANCE

The most obvious and well-known Christian symbol is the cross. It represents the death and resurrection of Jesus. Churches often display a cross in a centralized location. You may also see the cross in artwork or worn as jewelry.

The dove is another important symbol that represents the Holy Spirit. In fact, a dove appeared when Jesus was baptized. Matthew 3:16 says, "As soon as Jesus was baptized, He went up out of the water. At that moment heaven was opened, and He saw the Spirit of God descending like a dove and alighting on him."

Other Christian symbols were developed in secret to help early Christians find each other. The ichthys, which most people now call the "Jesus fish," dates back to the first century. During that time, Rome viewed Christianity as a cult instead of a true religion. Christians hid their faith and worshipped in secret to protect themselves.

The next time you're at church, take a close look at your surroundings. You'll probably see at least a few symbols. If you notice any you don't recognize on your own, ask someone to explain them to you.

[69]
WORSHIP PRACTICES AROUND THE WORLD: DIVERSE EXPRESSIONS OF FAITH

As Christianity spread around the world, many regions added in parts of their own cultures and customs. This could include extra celebrations around a local holiday or recognizing a particular person with a special link to a certain area.

For instance, Catholics in Vietnam celebrate the Feast of Our Lady of La Vang on November 22. This holiday remembers how the Virgin Mary and two angels appeared to a group of Catholics in 1798 while they were hiding from persecution. The Virgin Mary comforted the group and told them how to heal themselves using leaves from the forest. The Lady of La Vang is one of the patron saints of Vietnam.

Similarly, Ireland honors its patron saint, St. Patrick, every year with festivities and parades. Celebrations typically include food, music, and drinking. It's also common for people to wear a shamrock since St. Patrick used the shamrock to explain the idea of the holy trinity when he first brought Christianity to Ireland.

It's also common for different countries to have unique Christmas traditions. In Ukraine, families eat a full meal with 12 courses to celebrate the 12 apostles. In the Philippines, Christians celebrate by creating colorful lanterns out of paper and bamboo. These lanterns are decorated with stars to represent the star of Bethlehem.

If you're interested in learning more about different cultural traditions, consider bringing it up during youth group, Sunday school, or Bible study. Various members of your congregation may have their own cultural traditions to share. Even if you don't have any firsthand experiences to contribute, you can still do research and help others learn more about different cultural beliefs from around the world.

CHAPTER FOURTEEN:
APOLOGETICS & DEFENDING YOUR FAITH

Think of apologetics as a type of discussion where Christians defend their beliefs and express their ideas about faith. It can be frustrating when someone questions your faith or makes fun of your religion. Instead of lashing out or yelling, try to stay calm when you talk to others about God. Getting into a heated argument or saying hurtful things won't convince the other person to listen. Remember that religion is a sensitive topic, and a lot of people have beliefs that are different from yours.

Peter 3:15 says, "But in your hearts honor Christ the Lord as holy, always being prepared to make a defense to anyone who asks you for a reason for the hope that is in you; yet do it with gentleness and respect." Someone who's questioning your faith might actually be struggling with their own doubts. Showing them kindness and standing firm in your beliefs can convince them to be more open to God.

You never know when you could be the person who changes someone's mind and helps them see the truth about God. Instead of jumping to conclusions or getting angry, do your best to handle objections with kindness.

[70]
WHAT IS APOLOGETICS: THE BASICS

At a basic level, apologetics is simply defending Christianity with arguments and reason. The purpose of apologetics is to protect the truth of God's message. This might involve responding to people who criticize Christianity or claim that God isn't real. It could also mean correcting others when they say things about God that aren't true.

People who engage in apologetics are called *apologists*. For instance, William Paley was a writer, Anglican priest, and apologist who's known for his theories of God's existence. His works include *Natural Theology; or Evidences of the Existence and Attributes of the Deity,* and *View of the Evidences of Christianity.*

[71]
COMMON OBJECTIONS TO CHRISTIANITY: HOW TO RESPOND

There are thousands of different religions around the world. Not everyone believes in Christianity and its teachings. Some people don't follow any religion at all. Because of this, you may hear different objections to God and Christianity.

Some people state claim there isn't enough physical evidence that Jesus existed. However, proving that someone really lived isn't as easy as it might sound. Jesus was born thousands of years ago before the age of camera phones, the internet, and even the widespread use of paper. Records were often passed along verbally as stories instead of written down or saved. Plus, everyday artifacts from that long ago are rare.

Another issue that people bring up is the existence of pain and suffering. You might hear others say that if God really existed, there wouldn't be so many terrible things in the world. The response to that is simple: free will. God gave humans the ability to make our own choices, and that includes making decisions that hurt others. Suffering is just proof of free will. It doesn't mean that God isn't real.

You'll also meet people who want more scientific proof that God exists before they'll believe in Christianity. Trusting in God, even though we can't see Him ourselves, is simply a part of faith. You won't be able to produce the proof that others are looking for, but you can explain more about why you believe and how you know for sure that God is really there.

These are just a few examples of objections you might hear from those who don't believe. You won't always be able to change someone's mind, but it's a good idea to practice how you might respond to these objections. This way, if a friend has questions about your faith or how to overcome doubt, you'll already have a few ideas to bring up.

[72]
HISTORICAL EVIDENCE FOR JESUS: KEY POINTS

There are countless pieces of historical evidence that document Jesus's life. Written records from that time reference Jesus's life and works. Besides Christian documents, there are also records from Jewish and Roman sources.

Many churches around the world have relics that are said to date back to the time of Jesus. Famous items include the Shroud of Turin and Veil of Veronica. The Catholic Church even has pieces of the True Cross from the crucifixion. The pieces are currently stored in Rome at the Basilica of the Holy Cross in Jerusalem.

Researchers will likely find more historical evidence in the future. In 2006, the Nazareth Archaeological Project began to dig underneath the Sisters of Nazareth Convent. Researchers knew there was a structure underneath the convent. It was first discovered in 1880, but no one had ever explored it. Archaeologists also found other buildings and homes nearby in the same area.

It's possible that Jesus lived in the home during His childhood. In the seventh century, Adomnán of Iona wrote that Jesus's home was located in between two tombs. He also described the two nearby churches. These details have helped archaeologists understand the layout of Nazareth during Jesus's early years.

[73]
SCIENTIFIC EVIDENCE: SUPPORTING THE EXISTENCE OF GOD

It isn't always clear how science and religion fit together, but they aren't as different as people think. The more we learn about the universe, the more it's clear that everything fits together. If you changed even one tiny scientific principle, our entire universe could fall apart. Theoretical physicist Stephen Hawking once wrote, "The remarkable fact is that the values of these numbers seem to have been very finely adjusted to make possible the development of life."

If science seems to contradict the existence of God, who knows that we've found the right answer? Our understanding of the universe and scientific principles is constantly changing. Once upon a time, scientists believed that seizures were caused by demons. Obviously, we now know that isn't the case. It often takes time and technological advancements to learn that we were wrong about one idea or another.

[74]
MORAL ARGUMENTS FOR THE EXISTENCE OF GOD

Moral arguments consider the role of right and wrong. Since people have a shared sense of good and evil, it makes sense that there's a larger order to the universe. For example, you don't have to tell someone that it's wrong to hurt another person or take something that doesn't belong to them. Everyone understands why those actions are bad.

Christians who use moral arguments to support the existence of God believe that this idea of right and wrong comes from God. It explains why people from different cultures, countries, and backgrounds have some of the same values. Plus, most people will agree that it's easy to see evidence of evil deeds in the world around us. If there's evil, then there must also be good.

[75]
PHILOSOPHICAL ARGUMENTS FOR THE EXISTENCE OF GOD

One of the most popular arguments for the existence of God is that our universe just makes sense on a basic level. Whether it's birds migrating south for the winter or the sun rising every day, there's a pattern and an order to the world. If God didn't design all these incredible things, how could they possibly have formed on their own?

William Paley compared the universe to a watch. Imagine that you've never seen a watch before in your life. If you suddenly found one and looked at the complicated parts inside, you'd probably assume that someone invented it. It's just too complex to be made by chance or coincidence. That was Paley's entire point about the creation of the universe.

A second argument builds on the idea that everything has a cause. Nothing happens spontaneously without a reason. If you sniff a flower and sneeze, it's because you had a reaction to the pollen. If you miss the bus, you'll probably be late to school. These are simple examples, but they show that everything in life has a cause and an effect.

If you go all the way back to the start of the universe, there had to be a first cause that sparked the entire chain of events. Some philosophers argue that God must have been the first cause. He decided how the universe would look at the start of all life. Now, all these years later, we can make our own decisions and cause things to happen as well.

The French philosopher René Descartes has yet another theory that God exists because so many humans have an idea of who God is. Descartes claimed that we only have a sense of God because He exists and created us. Otherwise, humans wouldn't have any ideas about God or a perfect being existing in the universe.

The existence of God is one of the most important philosophical questions. There are dozens of philosophical arguments about why God exists. You may get the chance to learn about philosophers and their theories in school. If not, it's worth looking them up on your own to understand more about how people in other time periods understood God.

CHAPTER FIFTEEN:
PROPHECIES & REVELATIONS

The Bible is full of prophecies and hints about the future. Some of these have already happened, while others have yet to happen. Only God knows exactly when prophecies will be fulfilled and how each event will take place.

Certain prophecies even address the end of the world as we know it. The Book of Revelation holds many of these details. We'll explain these prophecies in basic terms, but you'll need to keep studying the Bible to fully understand them.

[76]
OLD TESTAMENT PROPHECIES: FULFILLED IN JESUS

The birth of Jesus fulfilled the Old Testament prophecies about the Messiah. Isaiah said that the Messiah would be born to a virgin. The prophet Micah stated that the birth would take place in Bethlehem. Hundreds of years later, their prophecies came true when the Virgin Mary gave birth to Jesus.

Other Old Testament prophecies spoke of how the Messiah would be betrayed by a friend and die with criminals as a sacrifice. Jesus's life followed these predictions too. Christians view these prophecies as proof that Jesus is the Messiah. Jews, on the other hand, don't believe that Jesus fulfilled the messianic prophecies.

[77]
REVELATION: AN OVERVIEW OF THE BOOK

The Book of Revelation is the last book in the New Testament. It contains messages to seven churches and describes visions that signal the second coming of Jesus. Revelation also contains a message of hope that good will win over evil.

In Revelation 2:10, Jesus says to the church in Smyrna, "Do not be afraid of what you are about to suffer. I tell you, the devil will put some of you in prison to test you, and you will suffer persecution for ten days. Be faithful, even to the point of death, and I will give you life as your victor's crown."

Don't worry if this seems confusing. The Book of Revelation is one of the most complicated parts of the Bible. If you have specific questions, ask someone you trust to explain it to you or bring it up in Bible study.

[78]
END TIMES:
WHAT CHRISTIANS BELIEVE

Revelation tells us that after the return of Jesus, He will reign for 1,000 years. At that point, God will destroy Earth as we know it and create a New Earth and a New Heaven. Anyone who believes in Jesus will go to Heaven during the Rapture. The rest will face God's judgment if they still refuse to accept Jesus.

Therefore, Revelation isn't actually predicting "the end of the world." It just explains what will happen as we approach the next phase of God's plan. It's also a promise that God will reward anyone who trusts in Him and punish those who embrace evil.

[79]
SECOND COMING OF CHRIST:
KEY TEACHINGS

No one knows exactly when Jesus will return. One of the key signs is that a false messiah will rise to power. 2 Thessalonians 2:4 says, "He will oppose and will exalt himself over everything that is called God or is worshiped, so that he sets himself up in God's temple, proclaiming himself to be God."

After the Antichrist appears, there will be a Great Tribulation. The world will experience more natural disasters, wars, and suffering. There will also be false prophets who spread lies and persecute anyone who doesn't agree. In Matthew 24:4–5, Jesus tells the disciples, "Watch out that no one deceives you. For many will come in my name, claiming, 'I am the Messiah,' and will deceive many."

Jesus warned His followers not to trust rumors that He has returned. People will claim that the Messiah has arrived, but it will be a lie. When Jesus truly returns, He will send angels, and there will be trumpets to announce His presence.

[80]
HEAVEN & HELL:
UNDERSTANDING ETERNAL LIFE

Before Adam and Eve sinned against God, they weren't doomed to die. They betrayed God's trust when they ate the forbidden fruit. Jesus's death saved humanity by giving us a second chance at a new relationship with God. John 3:16 says, "For God so loved the world that He gave His one and only Son, that whoever believes in Him shall not perish but have eternal life."

The Bible describes Heaven as a beautiful, peaceful place. The faithful who go to Heaven won't have to worry about earthly problems like pain, fear, or hunger. The New Jerusalem will have streets of gold and gates made of pearl. A river with the water of life flows through the streets. It will be completely unlike anything we've seen on Earth.

Hell, by comparison, is full of suffering and misery. In Matthew 13:41–42, Jesus says, "The Son of Man will send out his angels, and they will weed out of his kingdom everything that causes sin and all who do evil. They will throw them into the blazing furnace, where there will be weeping and gnashing of teeth." Just as Heaven is eternal, so is Hell.

CHAPTER SIXTEEN:
LIVING WITH PURPOSE

Living with purpose sounds complicated, but it's really just about following your dreams and doing your best to understand what God has in store for you. While you won't know everything He has planned, your natural gifts are a big clue about what you're meant to do. Take some time to think about what makes you feel happy and fulfilled.

If you don't know what you want to do after high school, don't panic just yet. Some people don't find their calling until later in life. It may take a little more life experience before you discover all your passions and talents. Just think back to the story of Dorothy Day. She didn't even become a Christian until she was already an adult, but she made a lasting impact on Christianity.

[81]
GOD'S PURPOSE FOR YOUR LIFE: DISCOVERING IT

God has a purpose for all of us, but it takes work to discover your purpose in life. If you feel torn when you think about the future, try not to focus too much on what you think you're supposed to do. Social pressures and other distractions can get in the way of your true calling.

For example, it's common for people to focus too much on making money instead of following their passions and gifts. Before long, you end up motivated by greed instead of doing your best to understand what God intended for you. Proverbs 19:21 says, "Many are the plans in a person's heart, but it is the Lord's purpose that prevails."

Before you make a decision about your future, ask yourself why you want to follow a certain path. Do you believe it's what God would want you to do, or are you actually motivated by something else? Being honest about your motivations makes it easier to see when you're heading in the wrong direction.

[82]
SPIRITUAL GIFTS: IDENTIFYING & USING THEM

Christians receive spiritual gifts from the Holy Spirit to spread the word of God. The Bible describes all sorts of spiritual gifts. For instance, Romans 12:6–8 lists the following:

- Prophecy: speaking God's messages and comforting others
- Serving: helping people in a selfless way
- Teaching: explaining God's messages to others
- Encouragement: motivating others to spiritually grow
- Giving: providing resources to the church and people in need
- Leadership: organizing within the church and guiding others
- Mercy: showing compassion and kindness to others

Do any of these sound like your spiritual gifts? It isn't hard to see examples of these gifts at work in your congregation. Running a food drive could represent giving and mercy. Leading a Sunday school lesson is a part of teaching and leadership. When you really take the time to think about everyone's skills, you'll see that God has given you everything you need to spread His message.

[83]
GOD'S CALLING: HOW TO DISCERN IT

If you're worried about hearing God's call, the simplest answer is to just listen. Instead of dwelling too much on what's going on in your life, take the time to put aside your worldly problems. Use those peaceful moments to pray and open yourself up to God.

Don't let distractions like school or sports get in the way of your relationship with God. If your life feels too busy, take a step back and think about what matters the most. Maybe you can reorganize your schedule to make more time for your faith. This could be as easy as waking up a few minutes earlier to pray in the peace and quiet before you start your day. If you don't take the time to listen to God, you won't be able to hear Him when he calls.

[84]
LIVING WITH INTEGRITY: BEING TRUE TO YOUR FAITH

It isn't always easy to do the right thing. No one likes to stand out from the group or feel like they don't fit in. However, staying true to God and your beliefs may not always be the popular decision. You'll face challenges where you have to choose between your faith and what everyone else is doing.

Pay close attention to who you're spending time with. The right friends won't pressure you to go against what you believe. They'll respect your faith in God even if they aren't Christians themselves. While you can't control who sits next to you in school or who else joins the basketball team, you do get to decide which relationships to invest in.

If you make a mistake, it doesn't mean that you aren't a good Christian. Everyone has regrets about the past. The key is to learn from what happened and avoid slipping up the next time you're in that situation. God knows that we aren't perfect. Being willing to admit when you're wrong and make healthy changes is a huge step toward living with integrity.

[85]
MAKING AN IMPACT: USING YOUR LIFE FOR GOD'S GLORY

You don't need to be a famous missionary or a priest to dedicate yourself to God's glory. Just being a good Christian is enough. Remember that even small acts like inviting a friend to church or offering to pray with a loved one can make an enormous difference in someone's life.

Honoring God also sets a good example for others. People will see that you're dedicated to God and want to follow in your footsteps. You never know when someone will notice your faithfulness and decide to change their own relationship with God for the better.

Only you can decide exactly how you want to help and make a difference in the world around you. When you see an opportunity to act, don't let the fear of failure get in the way. God gave you gifts and talents that are totally unique to you. Use those to spread His message and lead others down the right path.

CHAPTER SEVENTEEN:
DEALING WITH LIFE'S HARDSHIPS

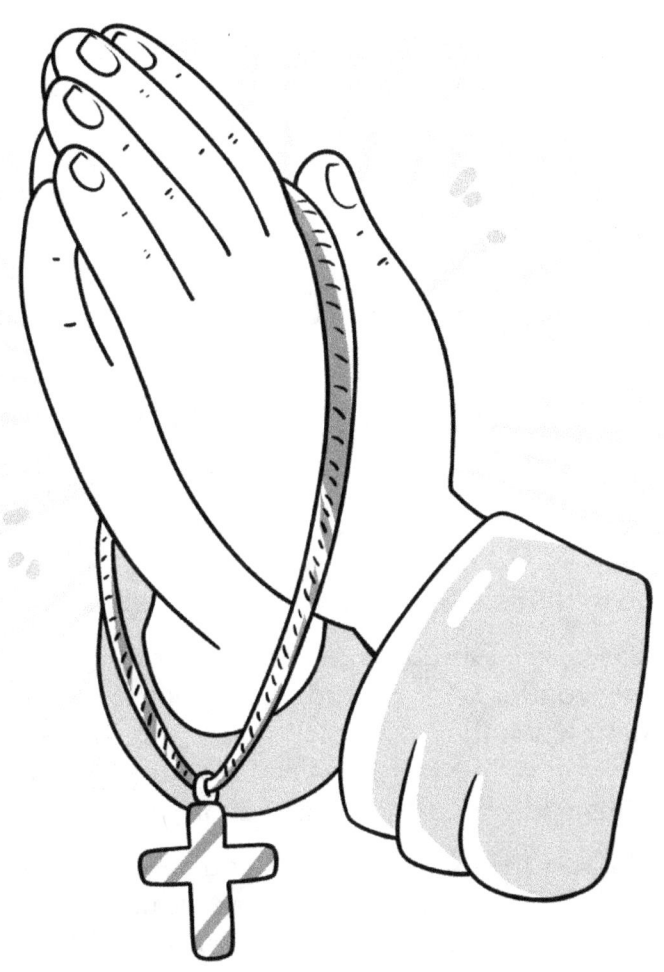

No matter what you do, life has its ups and downs. Whether you're dealing with a major tragedy or a small hiccup, it's still important to have healthy coping mechanisms. Otherwise, negative emotions like sadness or anger can grow out of control.

Fortunately, you don't have to deal with hardships on your own. Remember that you always have God and your congregation at your back when you're feeling lost or confused. Plus, your loved ones and friends want to see you heal and succeed.

It might seem like everyone is always put together all the time, but that isn't true. People act differently on social media or in public. In reality, everyone needs help at one point or another. There's nothing wrong with admitting that you're upset, confused, or uncertain about the future. The last thing you should do is try to tackle a huge problem by yourself.

[86]
LOSS & GRIEF: FINDING COMFORT IN GOD

Death is a natural part of life, but it still isn't easy when you lose a loved one. You'll probably feel a mix of emotions, including sadness, anger, and guilt. Instead of ignoring these emotions, take some time to think about why you're feeling them.

In some cases, grief and loss can even make you angry with God. You might wonder why He didn't let your loved one live longer or heal them when they were sick. These are all natural feelings to have when you're in pain. The key is to turn toward God in these moments instead of shutting Him out of your life.

Talk to God and pray about what you're going through. God is always ready to listen. Sharing your thoughts and feelings through prayer can help you work through your grief. 2 Corinthians 1:3-4 says, "Praise be to the God and Father of our Lord Jesus Christ, the Father of compassion and the God of all comfort, who comforts us in all our troubles so that we can comfort those in any trouble with the comfort we ourselves receive from God."

[87]
ANXIETY & DEPRESSION: SEEKING HELP & GOD'S PEACE

Everyone feels anxious or down from time to time. It's totally normal to be anxious if you have to read a story in front of the class or ask someone to a school dance. However, ongoing anxiety and depression can turn into more serious mental health problems.

People who have chronic anxiety often feel worried about the future and stressed about things they can't control. Symptoms may include trouble sleeping, shortness of breath, and dizziness. Depression, meanwhile, leads to a sense of dread and hopelessness.

If you're struggling to deal with your anxiety and depression, you don't have to fight that battle alone. Your parents/guardians, teachers, friends, and congregation are all part of your support system. It's okay to lean on them when you don't know where to turn.

You may even need to speak with a professional who's trained in counseling and mental health. Your school guidance counselor is a great place to start. They can work with you directly or recommend other resources in your community. If you feel more comfortable in your church, try talking to a Sunday school teacher or another leader about getting help.

As you're dealing with anxiety and depression, make sure to let any mental health professionals know that your faith is an important part of your life. They can figure out ways to use prayer in your treatment plan.

[88]
BULLYING:
RESPONDING WITH GOD'S LOVE

When someone is bullying you, it may feel impossible to respond with love, but that's what Jesus taught us to do. In Matthew 5:43–45, He says, "You have heard that it was said, 'Love your neighbor and hate your enemy.' But I tell you, love your enemies and pray for those who persecute you, that you may be children of your Father in heaven."

The key is to look for the best in people and offer forgiveness even when someone has hurt you in the past. Holding onto negative emotions will only make you angrier. Letting go allows love to replace any anger or pain. Showing love to bullies also means that you're praying for your enemy to change and become a better person in the future.

At the same time, showing love to your enemies doesn't mean that you have to tolerate abuse. If someone is hurting or threatening you, get an adult involved as soon as possible. You don't have to confront a bully on your own, especially if you don't feel safe. You can still show love to an enemy while taking steps to protect yourself.

[89]
FAMILY ISSUES:
NAVIGATING THEM WITH FAITH

Every family has its share of problems. Instead of arguing or ignoring an issue, you can use your faith to find a solution. If the problem has to do with a specific topic, check to see what the Bible has to say about it. Although the Bible was written a long time ago, many of its stories and lessons are still relevant today.

Even if you just pray together and ask God for guidance, you're still putting in the work to make your family stronger. You won't always figure out an answer right away, but the fact that you're trying shows that you all care. Praying will also remind you to be humble instead of only focusing on what you want. Look for ways to compromise with your loved ones and think about what God would expect you to do in your situation.

If your family can't get past an issue, you may be able to get counseling through your church. Your pastor or priest can sit with you and give advice about how to heal as a family. They may also be able to offer a neutral opinion as someone who isn't directly involved in the situation. Hearing another person's thoughts can help you see when you're being stubborn, selfish, or unforgiving.

[90]
SELF-ESTEEM:
SEEING YOURSELF AS GOD SEES YOU

Self-esteem is how you view yourself and your worth as a person. Everyone feels down about themselves sometimes, but it's important to get back on your feet even after a setback. If you fail a test or you don't get picked for the school play, don't be too hard on yourself. It doesn't mean you won't be successful when you try again in the future.

When you're feeling down, remember that God designed you as a unique individual. No one else on the planet has exactly the same gifts, dreams, and skills as you. Appreciating who you are is a way to show your gratitude to God. Psalm 139:13–14 says, "For you created my inmost being; you knit me together in my mother's womb. I praise you because I am fearfully and wonderfully made; your works are wonderful, I know that full well."

CHAPTER EIGHTEEN: ETERNAL PERSPECTIVE

It's hard to think about eternity when our lives are so short by comparison. Even so, it's important to remember God's promises and put daily life into perspective. Something that seems terrible now probably won't seem so awful in a year or two. Even the excitement of major successes will fade with time.

When you think about eternity instead of just the life you're living now, it's easier to keep things in perspective. Being content with the plan God has for you can help you think clearly and stay calm even when there's a lot going on in your everyday life. It means that no matter what happens, you trust in Jesus Christ and the promise of eternal life.

[91]
WHO WE ARE
AFTER DEATH

The Bible tells us that we'll be able to recognize our loved ones even after death. Luke 16:19–31 tells the story of a rich man and a beggar named Lazarus. The rich man is selfish and ends up going to Hell. Lazarus, meanwhile, goes to Heaven.

The rich man looks up from Hell and sees Abraham and Lazarus. He begs Abraham to help him. Abraham replies, "…between us and you, a great chasm has been set in place so that those who want to go from here to you cannot, nor can anyone cross over from there to us." This story shows that people still know each other even after death, but no one is allowed to cross between Heaven and Hell.

[92]
REWARDS IN HEAVEN:
WHAT THE BIBLE SAYS

The Bible says that Heaven is a paradise with no fear, sorrow, or negative emotions. Instead of night and day, Heaven is always shining with the light of God and His angels. It's the ultimate reward for Christians who follow God and believe in the love of Jesus.

However, that doesn't mean you should only follow God's rules because you hope to have a reward in Heaven. Your motivations matter just as much as your actions. After all, if you're doing a good deed for a selfish reason, is it really a good deed? Instead of focusing on getting into Heaven, you should be praying and helping others because it's the Christian thing to do.

[93]
LIVING WITH ETERNITY IN MIND: HOW IT CHANGES EVERYTHING

When you think about eternity instead of just the present, you'll realize how important your everyday decisions really are. Every choice is an opportunity to live your life according to God. If you feel like you're heading in the wrong direction, stop and think about what kind of person you want to be.

Keeping eternity in mind can also make it easier to help other people. When you know someone is going through a hard time, do your best to guide and support them. You could be the reason your friend or classmate ends up finding Jesus.

Lastly, day-to-day sacrifices won't seem so bad when you compare them to the promise of eternal life. If someone is bullying you for your faith or you have to miss a school event to go to church, remember that eternity is bigger than just those moments. As 1 John 2:17 says, "The world and its desires pass away, but whoever does the will of God lives forever."

[94]
HOPE:
HOLDING ONTO IT IN ALL CIRCUMSTANCES

Hope can help you get through tough situations in your life. Remember that God is always watching out for you, even when you're afraid or uncertain about what to do. Just look to the Bible for inspiration.

1 Samuel 17 tells the story of David and Goliath. During the battle, David held onto the hope that God would protect him. He said, "You come against me with sword and spear and javelin, but I come against you in the name of the Lord Almighty, the God of the armies of Israel, whom you have defied." In the end, David defeated Goliath even though all the odds were against him. He never lost hope.

Knowing that God is behind you and supporting you will give you the strength to keep going. Plus, hope quickly spreads from one person to the next. When you know that everything will turn out okay, it's reassuring to other people in the same situation.

[95]
JOY:
FINDING IT IN GOD

There's so much to celebrate when you fully accept God's love. It means that God accepts and loves you for who you are. You can express your joy in many ways. This could include singing in the choir, acting in the church play, or just praying about how you're feeling.

When there are festivals or holidays, take the chance to celebrate God and show how happy you are to be part of His flock. Sharing your joy allows you to connect with others in your life and remember the Christians who came before. It also shows people who are on the fence about Christianity that there's so much happiness, peace, and love waiting for them.

CHAPTER NINETEEN:
GOD'S PROMISES

Whether it was leading the Israelites out of Egypt or telling Noah that He wouldn't send another flood, God has always kept His promises. Biblical stories show that amazing things are possible when you trust in God and believe that He will follow through.

God promised Abraham that he would have an enormous family with as many children in his line as there were stars in the sky. Abraham and his wife Sarah were confused because they were too old to have children. Even though they doubted that it was possible, God fulfilled His promise. They had their son Isaac when Sarah was 90 years old, and Abraham was 100.

[96]
GOD'S FAITHFULNESS: TRUSTING HIS PROMISES

You may doubt when your brother promises to let you pick the family movie next time, or your friend swears that they won't tell anyone else a secret, but you can always trust in God's promises. Numbers 23:19 reminds us, "God is not human, that He should lie, not a human being, that He should change his mind."

However, you won't always know when or how those promises will be fulfilled. Even though you might be curious, there are some things we aren't meant to know. God shared many parts of His plan with us, which you can read about in the Bible. The rest will happen when it's the right time.

[97]
PROVISION: GOD'S PROMISE TO PROVIDE

God has always provided for humanity. When He created the universe, He made everything we need to survive. In addition to basic needs like food and water, God provides for us spiritually as well. He gave us free will to make our own choices and the gifts we need to spread the Gospel.

Matthew 6:25–26 reminds us not to worry about material things because God will make sure we have enough: "Therefore I tell you, do not worry about your life, what you will eat or drink; or about your body, what you will wear. Is not life more than food and the body more than clothes? Look at the birds of the air; they do not sow or reap or store away in barns, and yet your heavenly Father feeds them."

[98]
PROTECTION:
GOD'S PROMISE TO PROTECT

God promises to protect us from evil and watch over us. This doesn't mean that your life will be perfect or that nothing bad can ever happen. Christians still have problems and hardships, but God doesn't expect you to get through those moments alone.

In Isaiah 54:17, God says, "No weapon forged against you will prevail, and you will refute every tongue that accuses you. This is the heritage of the servants of the Lord, and this is their vindication from me." When you're feeling scared or threatened, remember that God is there to protect and support you no matter what.

[99]
PRESENCE:
GOD'S PROMISE TO ALWAYS
BE WITH US

God is with each and every one of us. In Isaiah 41:10, God says, "So do not fear, for I am with you; do not be dismayed, for I am your God. I will strengthen you and help you; I will uphold you with my righteous right hand."

You don't need to worry that God will abandon you. He is always there to hear your prayers and guide you in your daily life. Even if you can't sense that God is with you or you don't feel like you deserve His love, He will still be right beside you. That's His promise.

[100]
ETERNAL LIFE:
GOD'S PROMISE FOR THE FUTURE

There's no way to know exactly what the future will hold. All you can do is make the best decisions possible with the information you have now. As you get ready to graduate from high school and start your adult life, think about the kind of Christian you want to be now that you're more independent.

Talk to your pastor and other members of your congregation. They can help guide you in the right direction. This way, you'll know you're making smart choices about your everyday life without straying from what God intends for you. The last thing you want to do is risk your chance at eternal life because you let ordinary temptations get in the way.

Fortunately, you have a lot of time ahead of you to map out who you want to be as you get older. You already have a head start just from embracing God and making your faith a priority. As long as you don't lose sight of that, you're well on your way to keeping your promises to God and earning what He has promised in return.

CONCLUSION

Congratulations on reaching the end of this book. By now, you should have a better understanding of your faith and what it means to be a Christian. We started out by talking about God's existence and how to build a relationship with God. From there, we discussed Christian values and Jesus's teachings. You also learned about the Holy Spirit, the history of the church, and how to deepen your personal faith.

In the following chapters, we explained the different theories and arguments for the existence of God. You read about famous philosophers and their views on faith. Next, we talked about prophecies and revelations in the Bible. This included a discussion about eternal life and what happens after the Second Coming of Jesus.

Lastly, we introduced what it means to have an eternal perspective and trust in God's promises. While we didn't cover everything there is to know about God, this book covered many of the key concepts and lessons you need to know. If you want to learn more about a particular topic, you can do your own research, look up passages in the Bible, or start a dialogue in your youth group. Plus, even after you're no longer a teenager, you can still come back to this book any time you have questions.

[101]
FINAL ENCOURAGEMENT: STAYING STRONG IN YOUR FAITH

At your age, you have your whole life ahead of you. Before long, you'll find a career or go off to college. Along the way, you'll face all sorts of new experiences and challenges. Your faith, however, doesn't have to change. It can be a constant in your life even as you move away, make new friends, or fall in love.

If you start to feel like your faith isn't as strong as it should be, go back to the basics. Make time in your schedule to pray and read the Bible. Spend more time in church with your congregation.

You'll slowly rebuild the habits you had before and feel your faith grow again. God will always welcome you back with open arms.

Remember to keep learning and showing love to everyone you meet. As a Christian, you belong to a global family with millions of people. Together, there's so much we can accomplish. Whenever you're unsure about the future, or you need a word of encouragement, just think about what Jesus said in Matthew 19:26: "…with God, all things are possible."

www.ingramcontent.com/pod-product-compliance
Lightning Source LLC
Chambersburg PA
CBHW061650120626
46550CB00003B/891